Building An Evangelistic Church

By Paul W. Powell

As a part of Bold Mission Thrust, Southern Baptists
will engage in a great evangelistic program in 1995.
The theme will be "Here's Hope! Share Jesus Now."
This book will help pastors and staff members prepare
themselves and their churches for maximum success.

D1027299

Annuity Board of the Southern Baptist Convention
Dallas, Texas
Copyright ©1991

Building An Evangelistic Church

Dedication

*To every person who will
find Christ as Savior
because some reader
witnesses to His love.*

Preface

When someone once suggested that rowing become part of Clemson University's athletic program, then Athletic Director, Frank Howard, declared, "We aren't gonna have no sport where you sit down and go backwards" (Reader's Digest).

In God's work, there is no place for sitting down and going backward either. David Livingston said, "I'm ready to go anywhere so long as it's forward."

God spoke to Moses as he stood between Pharaoh's pursuing army and the Red Sea: "Wherefore criest thou unto me, speak to the people that they go forward."

Today, God's people need to be challenged to go forward. In spite of the enemies behind us and the obstacles before us, go forward to build bigger and better churches. We simply cannot accomplish this with a maintenance mentality. The local church deserves our highest and best energies, for the church is the means through which God has chosen to do his work in the world.

But how do we build a great evangelistic church? There are no easy answers, no quick fixes. If you truly want to know what it takes, then I urge you to read on.

Our long and rich heritage of revival meetings has given birth to the custom of "going forward" publicly to confess that Christ is Savior. We need to do this only once. But the exhilaration of "going forward" should be relived again and again in the lives of others that we win. Certainly, it is all right at times to look back, but if we all make a commitment to go forward, we will realize God's plan.

Table of Contents

1

Build An Evangelistic Church

Television commentator, Dick Vermeil, covering an NFL game, made the observation: "You can't fire a cannon from a canoe." Instantly, the picture of an unstable, lightweight canoe bearing a huge Civil War cannon flashed through my mind. The scene was ludicrous, for I knew immediately what would happen if the cannon were fired. The recoil would be so powerful that it would tip the canoe and sink it.

Vermeil was referring to the game of football. He pointed out that running backs must have strong legs to get a fast start, break tackles, and slice through holes in the line.

I thought of it, however, in relation to the church, for it is as true ecclesiastically as it is athletically. You can't fire a cannon from a canoe. The church of Jesus Christ is not in the popgun or peashooter business. Our task is to fire "gospel cannon shots" heard around the world. To do this, we must have strong churches.

The mission of the church is clear, and Jesus left no doubt about it at his Ascension. When his disciples asked, "Lord, will you at this time restore again the kingdom to Israel?" Jesus answered, "It is not for you to know the times or the seasons, which the Father hath put in his own power. But ye shall receive power, after that the Holy Ghost is come upon you: and ye shall be witnesses unto me both in Jerusalem, and in all Judea, and in Samaria, and unto the uttermost part of the earth" (Acts 1:7-8).

Notice the disciples' concern for the "end time," but the Lord's concern for the "mean time." Some things never seem to change.

11

As Vance Havner suggested, there are many Christians today who spend their time trying to decipher the meaning of the fourth toe on the right foot of some obscure beast in prophecy, yet never use their own feet to cross the street and witness to a neighbor.

Are you an "end-time" Christian or a "mean-time" Christian? The major emphasis should remain where our Lord put it—on evangelism—not on eschatology. World evangelization is our generation's task, and we must not allow ourselves to be side-tracked. And to accomplish our mission, we must have great evangelistic churches. How do we build them? I offer seven suggestions.

1. Have a clear sense of purpose.
2. Pastor the people.
3. Build a warm and loving fellowship.
4. Develop an alive, spirited worship service.
5. Follow the time-tested laws of Sunday school growth.
6. Take a supermarket approach to ministry.
7. Have a passion for action.

Learn a Lesson from the Chicken Yard

First, have a clear sense of purpose. Olan Hendricks, a church management expert, noted that, any Christian organization in existence for more than 20 years usually has no goals, just activities.

It happens all the time. Long after a church loses sight of its purpose, they continue to organize meetings and create programs. They substitute activities for objectives.

Yet activity alone is not a sign of life. When I was growing up in East Texas, we often ate chicken, especially when guests came to visit. My mother would enter the yard, select the chicken she wanted to cook for dinner, take it by the neck, and with one hand twirl it around until its neck was broken. She would then drop it to the ground and wait for it to die. A chicken with a broken neck kicks, flaps its wings, and jerks its whole body until it dies.

In those few seconds, that chicken would be the most active bird in the barnyard, but it was also the one nearest death. Frantic activity was not that of life but of death. The same can be true of a church. For a church to be strong, all its activities and programs must focus on winning and discipling people for Jesus Christ.

Leadership Stems From Relationships

Second, pastor your people. Over the years I have written three books on church growth. Each of them emphasized the importance of the pastor being a strong leader. No great churches exist without strong leadership. However, I fear that some pastors have forgotten their calling. They act more like petty tyrants and dictators than servants of God and of the people. It is no surprise they are often in hot water.

Some of the most tragic words I have heard lately were spoken by a faithful and concerned lady about her church and her pastor. She remarked, "That man doesn't serve our church. Our church serves him."

I am a pastor at heart and preach almost every Sunday. Being a pastor means to love your people, to visit them in hospitals, nursing homes, and in their homes. You perform weddings, conduct funerals, and counsel. The caring pastor knows the hurts and needs of the church members and is available to them. With that type of relationship you can lead them: lead them as a shepherd, not drive them as a cowboy.

The best leadership always grows out of relationships. To lead people, a pastor must love them and move among them. Once he loses touch, he loses effectiveness as a leader. Spirit-attuned pastors help make great churches.

Acceptance Does Not Mean Approval

Third, build a warm, friendly fellowship where people immediately find love and acceptance. Remember that acceptance is not synonymous with approval. Jesus accepted the woman at the well. He did not approve of her five marriages and divorces or her live-in relationship with her boyfriend. He called her adultery what it was: sin. Because Jesus accepted her without judgment, he could tell her about the living water and see her life change forever.

If we are going to build great churches, our business is to throw ropes, not rocks. Today, most people don't choose or reject a church due to theology. Many don't even know theology. Instead, they go where they find love and acceptance. That doesn't mean theology is not important. It is important, but best learned in an atmosphere of agape love and acceptance.

One of America's greatest military heroes of World War I was Sergeant Alvin York. Raised in the hills of Tennessee, he was an expert marksman with both pistol and rifle. A deeply religious man, he was reluctant to go to war until his pastor persuaded him that it was his duty to do so.

During combat, his patrol was sent to silence a German machine gun nest. On that mission, Sergeant York alone killed 20 of the enemy and then forced a German major to surrender his entire command of 132 men. Sergeant York was awarded the Congressional Medal of Honor for that feat.

When asked how he did it, he replied, "I surrounded them!" We may not be able to surround that many people militarily. We can surely do it spiritually. All of us can reach out with arms of love and acceptance to capture an army of people for Jesus Christ.

Jesus declared, "He that cometh unto me I will in no wise cast out." We must give people that same assurance of acceptance, an essential ingredient for a great evangelistic church.

Make Worship a Celebration

Fourth, have an alive, spiritual worship service.

A vigorous church cannot resemble a morbid mausoleum. Its worship must be a celebration, expressing joy, hope, victory, and forgiveness, as well as reverence.

Methodist Bishop Arthur J. Moore told the story about a young minister who asked his bishop to hold a "quiet hour" in the young minister's church. The bishop responded, "What your church needs is not a quiet hour but an earthquake! I don't want to be as quiet as some of your people until I'm dead."

According to the late Vance Havner, "If things are quiet and undisturbed in your church, that is not necessarily a good sign. Things are usually pretty quiet around the sick and the dead and especially in graveyards."

Emotion is an integral part of life, so don't be afraid of it. After all, God gave us emotion as well as intellect, and we should worship him with both.

Someone once asked Mark Twain the secret of his success, and he replied, "I was born excited!" I wasn't born excited, but I was born-again excited. And I try to show it in almost everything I do, including my worship. The trouble with some churches, however, is that the bland lead the bland.

Remember that the Lord approves of neither idol worship nor idle worship. Leaving some worship services I feel like the little boy who went to "big church" for the first time. On the sanctuary wall hung a plaque in memory of young men of the congregation who died in the armed services. The plaque captured the boy's attention. In the middle of the service, he whispered to his mother, "What's that for?"

Hoping to quiet him with the answer, she replied, "It has been placed there in memory of the young men who died in the service."

The little boy responded, "Which service did they die in, the morning service or the evening?"

Harry Emerson Fosdick must have been thinking of such churches and services when he quipped, "The surprising thing is not that so few people come to church. The surprising thing is that anybody comes at all."

American frontier Christians shared a red-hot devotion to God. In other words, theirs was a singing, shouting, shining Holy Ghost religion. To be a member of their group meant suffering for the cause of Christ, sharing his message and shouldering his cross. It is doubtful that a church will ever be a great evangelistic church unless its worship embraces the joy and excitement of a celebration.

Offer a Lifeboat

Fifth, follow the time-tested laws of Sunday school growth. In building a church, we have two choices: we can build it on theatrics or we can build it on the basics.

A big church—but not a great one—can be built on theatrics. At the turn of the century, a well-known Fort Worth pastor built the biggest church in Texas, accomplished largely through his dynamic personality and high-powered promotion. On one occasion, he baptized a rodeo cowboy, allowing his horse on the platform as an observer.

Another time, the pastor announced a sensational sermon: "Should a Prominent Fort Worth Banker Buy High-Priced Silk Hose For Another Man's Wife?" As an added attraction, the sales clerk who sold the hosiery recounted her story. He then announced to the crowd, that since advertising his threat to expose the guilty banker, not one but three bankers came forward to confess! With the audience thus entertained, he turned to his sermon of the evening. When he had finished, the theatrical pastor jumped from the platform to a table on the main floor, imploring repentant sinners to come forward.

This pastor's church offered other benefits as well—a gymnasium and swimming pool!

Many churches build "performing arts centers" they call sanctuaries. We need to decide whether we want to operate a showboat or a lifeboat. After the fall of a celebrity pastor-evangelist, one of his followers lamented: "I'm getting tired of our church being a circus in front of the whole world." Indeed, a showboat runs out of steam after a while.

Building a church that rescues the perishing means giving attention to Sunday school and Bible study. Sunday school is not just another church organization. It is the church organized and functioning to carry out the Great Commission. The backbone of a strong church is a layperson teaching the Bible to a small, compatible class. More than a half-century ago, Arthur Flake gave us five time-tested laws for Sunday school growth: (1) know your possibilities; (2) enlarge the organization; (3) provide the space; (4) enlist and train the workers; and (5) go after the people.

Experience has proven that Flake was no fluke. His laws still work, and they remain essential to building a great evangelistic church.

Create a One-Stop Shop

Sixth, take a supermarket approach to ministry when possible. A big-city church that offers no more than Sunday school and worship will quickly be passed over. This may not sound "spiritual," but in most locales, it is important for you to provide more than the usual Sunday school and worship experiences. A pastor and staff must identify needs and develop ministries to meet them.

A few years ago I encountered Amish people for the first time. A deeply religious sect, the Amish reject virtually all modern ways. They dress in what many would call unfashionable clothes. They farm using old-fashioned methods and travel by primitive means. Up and down the highways you see them driving their horse-drawn, black buggies.

I noticed one modern feature on their buggies, however. Each one was equipped with two big red reflectors mounted on the rear. Apparently, so many of their buggies were being struck by cars and trucks that the government eventually required the reflectors for safety reasons.

By way of analogy, if our churches are striving to be great evangelistic churches, we choose modern vehicles to achieve this end—not horse and buggy methodology. In essence, we should be "anchored to the rock but geared to the times." Otherwise, we may be run over by progress.

Furthermore, we must identify special needs of people and then meet those needs. The more you are successful at meeting needs, the stronger the church will grow. If you have a youth program you will reach more youth. If you have a singles program you will reach more singles. In this highly specialized world, we should never stop thinking, growing or changing. If we do, the people will pass us by.

A church that becomes set in its ways, inflexible and rigid, will decline and become sterile. I have heard that the last words of a dying church are, "We never did it that way before."

Develop a Passion For Action

Seventh, have a passion for action. I love the Ebenezer Baptist

Church of Kansas City—although I have never seen it—because of its motto: "Wake up, pray up, sing up, preach up, pay up, and never give up, let up, back up, or shut up, until the cause of Christ is built up!"

Such intensity is necessary for growing strong churches. We are far more casual and nonchalant about God's work than we ought to be.

I speak in love, but I must say that some pastors will never have an evangelistic, growing church. They lack the intensity, the drive, the courage and the willingness to work, make the sacrifice and take the necessary risks. As Vance Havner said, "The tragedy of our times is that the situation is desperate but the saints are not." If the saints were as desperate as the situation, something might really happen. The scriptures portray the times in urgent terms that call for action.

Three weeks before President John F. Kennedy was assassinated, he said, "Almost all presidents leave office feeling that their work is unfinished. I have a lot to do, and so little time to do it." As pastors, we have a lot to do and little time to do it. There is an urgency about our task, and we must give ourselves to it. There will be ample time to sit and enjoy our inheritance in eternity. So go forward!

2

Reach Out To Every Person

Newspaper columnist Mike Burger wrote about a small boy who drew a valentine-shaped heart on the wall of the New York Public Library. Inside the heart, he inscribed this message: "Billy Meyer loves everybody!"

A slight variation of that message is what we preach. Our message was written by God, not by Billy Meyer. Our message is found in the Bible, not on a wall. But the message is essentially the same: "God loves everybody."

The universal thrust of the gospel permeates the scripture. Announcing he birth of Jesus, the angel declared, "Behold I bring you good tidings of great joy which shall be to all people..." According to Matthew's account of the Great Commission our Lord commanded, "Go ye therefore and teach all nations..." (Matthew 28:19). Mark's account reads, "Go ye into all the world, and preach the gospel to every creature" (Mark 16:15). All people! All nations! All the world! The good news is all-encompassing.

Far too often, however, our churches fail to share that great universal love; they have become narrow and exclusive. Vance Havner told of a church equipped with a sign that said: JESUS ONLY. One night, a storm smashed out the first three letters, leaving US ONLY. Too many churches think only of themselves, their needs, their convenience, their comfort. As a result, they become keepers of the aquarium rather than fishers of men.

As Christians, our mission is every person. And that is precisely what the Apostle Paul taught when he wrote of Jesus, " ... Whom we preach, warning every man, and teaching every man in all wisdom; that we may present every man perfect in Christ Jesus" (Colossians 1:28).

Paul thus explained his great mission and calling in life: to proclaim God's message of salvation through Jesus Christ, to warn every person, to teach every person, and to present every person perfect before God. In preceding verses as well, Paul twice declared he was "made a minister" of the gospel.

Paul neither founded the church at Colosse nor visited it. Nevertheless, he had a right to address the Christians there, and he wanted to make that clear. He told them his ministry was not an honor he bestowed upon himself, nor was it thrust upon him by other men. Instead, the Lord "made" him a minister. So it was on the basis of divine appointment that he spoke to them.

This gospel, Paul declares, centers on Jesus Christ, who died for all of humanity. The good news is that God's saving purpose does not encompass only an elected few. The gospel is intended for Gentiles and Jews alike (Colossians 1:27). Gentiles are admitted to salvation on equal terms with the Jews. The Messiah was not sent for Israel alone, but for all people, everywhere. Paul sums up the gospel: " ... which is Christ in you the hope of glory" (Colossians 1:27).

So it is not only the Christ of history or the biblical Christ who is our hope. Instead, hope comes through the "Christ in you!" The wonder of the gospel is that the Christ of history and the Christ of scripture—who lived, died, then rose again—can dwell in us. Through faith and commitment he enters our lives in personal, dynamic ways.

This indwelling Christ forgives our sins, makes people right with God, and eventually ushers us into heaven. Most important, he is available to all people everywhere.

Paul laid out his great mission and ours — fully to proclaim Christ to every human being. According to Paul, it is this indwelling Christ "Whom we preach, warning every man, and teaching every man; in all wisdom that we may present every person perfect in Christ Jesus..." (Colossians 1:28).

Earlier in this same chapter, Paul presented Christ as preeminent in the universe: above all and before all. In teaching "every man," Paul ultimately presents Christ as for all.

Paul's most significant contribution to Christianity was the introduction of Christ to the Gentiles, destroying forever the idea that God's love and mercy were reserved for one people or one nation. He confronted men with the conviction that Christ was for Gentile and Jew alike.

Sharing Christ with others in evangelistic witness is the heart of the church's task. A church which fulfills God's purpose can testify with Paul: "Him we proclaim."

Note that Paul identifies "every man" three times in the passage, emphasizing the universality of the gospel. Exclusivity characterized false teachers.

In truth, Christ is the only person in this world who is for "everybody." There are gifts some people will never possess, privileges some will never enjoy, and heights many will never attain. But for every person—through the good news of the gospel—the love of God in Christ and the transforming power to bring holiness into a life are unconditional.

Not every person can be a great thinker, writer, student, preacher, singer, or speaker. For those who are color blind, the loveliness of art means little. And for those who are tone deaf, the glory of music is lost. One thing is sure, though: every human being can know Jesus Christ.

We should be committed, like Paul, to take the gospel out to "every man." And like Paul, our central aim, should be to warn, teach, and present each one complete in Christ. This is the supreme plan of God, and it should be ours.

Warn Every Person

Our first duty is to warn every person, for they are in eternal danger. They are lost.

Jesus emphasized the two roads of life. Only a few persons find the straight and narrow one, which leads to life. Many travel the broad road to destruction. The fact that the "road is broad" means people can walk on it loaded with baggage, yet without sacrifice. Although this road leads to hell, it is not marked "hell," for Satan never admits where a road ends. Instead, the road is mismarked "heaven," but really leads to hell. Most people travel the road to hell, but they are so busy enjoying the ride that they give no thought to what lies at the end.

Someone needs to stand as a flagman on the road to destruction to shout, "Danger ahead!" Being a Christian is not just a matter of right or wrong, good or bad, sweet or sour. Being a Christian is a matter of life and death, of heaven and hell. Because we know of the awesome, impending judgment of God, we cannot be content merely to be saved ourselves. We must devote ourselves, as Paul did, to the "divine imperative" of warning every man.

Warning has always been part of the mission of God's people. A watchman over the house of Israel, Ezekiel was empowered to warn the people to reject their wicked ways. If he did not, they would die as sinners, but their blood would be on his hands (Ezekiel 33:8).

The Apostle Paul summarized his ministry in Ephesus by saying, " ... by the space of three years I ceased not to warn every one night and day with tears" (Acts 20:31).

Even the rich man in hell begged Lazarus to go to his father's home and warn his five brothers, for fear they should come to that awful place of torment.

This is our primary work, but many churches have forsaken it for more pleasant pursuits. Jewish author and humorist, Harry Golden, stung the modern church when he said, "If I were faced today with the decision my ancestors faced—become a Christian or die—I would pick a church fast. There is nothing to offend me in many modern churches. The minister gives a sermon on juvenile delinquency once a week, then reviews a movie next week, then everyone goes downstairs and plays bingo. The first part of the church they build is the kitchen. Five hundred years from now people will dig up these churches, find the steam tables, and wonder what kind of sacrifices we performed."

Our primary work is ever and always the same—to warn everyone. The fact is, every Christian this side of heaven should be concerned about every lost person this side of hell. Richard Baxter once declared that "I preach as never to preach again—as a dying man to dying men." So must we. Some people shy away from this kind of preaching calling it "scare religion." But, as R. G. Lee said, "If I had not been afraid of hell I do not think I would have started for heaven."

Teach Every Person

Like Paul, we must teach everyone. "Warning" is evangelism; "teaching" is discipleship. The lost need to be saved, but the saved need to be taught.

Most Christians' spiritual pilgrimages undergo three phases: condemnation, salvation, and stagnation. Hence, the newly-saved may quickly settle into a pew, where they sit and sour until the second coming.

Salvation is an instant event, but growth and maturity are gradual and continual. It takes a series of trials, frequent testing, dedication to learning, to help a believer realize the ultimate conclusion: Christlikeness. It may take many years. "Everything that is great in life is the product of slow growth; the newer, the greater, and the higher, and nobler the work, the slower is its growth, and the surer its lasting success," says N. G. Jones.

Toadstools grow overnight. Squash grows in a few weeks. Mighty redwoods develop over centuries. The difference in lasting value is indisputable. J. B. Gambrell once noted, "Conversion is the end of the Christian life—but it is the front end." We must never be content merely to lead people to salvation. Instead, through discipling, we must nurture saved souls, transforming them into saints, servants, and soldiers.

There are some Christian circles that disdain education and glorify ignorance. This is part of a larger anti-establishment, anti-institutional, anti-intellectual mood based on the idea that the less you know, the more spiritual you are and the more faith you have.

That attitude has no place among us. We must continue to learn as long as we live. Dr. E. Y. Mullins preached on the importance of education. Afterward, a man remarked to him: "The way you talk, it sounds like God can't use an ignorant preacher." Dr. Mullins replied, "My brother, sure he can. That's the only kind he has. We are all ignorant, just in varying degrees. But he can't use our ignorance. He uses what we know, and the more you know the more he can use you."

Minutes later, this man was asked to pray. His prayer went something like this: "Lord, I thank you for my ignorance. Make me ignorant-er than a mule. Amen." When Dr. Mullins returned to the seminary, he addressed the faculty: "Brethren, that is one prayer I believe God answered before it was ever prayed."

I heard about a preacher who became carried away and confused during his sermon. He prayed, "Lord, eliminate my mind so I can deliver this sermon." To preach effectively, what we need is illumination—not elimination—of our minds.

Brains were God's idea; he expects us to use them. That's why he said, "Study [be diligent] to shew yourself approved unto God..."

John Wesley was right when he said, "God can use a sharp instrument better than a dull one." Teaching sharpens us for our greatest usefulness: winning the lost and teaching the saved. If we win the battle for evangelism but lose the battle for discipleship, we have lost the church for the next generation.

Present Every Person

As Paul, we are to present every person perfect (complete) in Jesus Christ. A reporter asked Pepper Martin, a former baseball player for the St. Louis Cardinals, "What is your chief ambition in life?"

"My chief ambition is to go to heaven," answered Martin.

When the newspaper reporter laughed, Martin responded: "That's not a funny matter. It is a final matter."

In Colossians, Paul observes the finality of all things and refers to the time when we shall all be accountable to God. Paul's consuming passion is to "present every man perfect in Christ" on that day.

In the passage, "present" literally means to stand beside, to recommend, to substantiate. Furthermore, the word "perfect" in the

Greek is *teleios*, meaning to be mature, complete, fully grown. In the end, Paul wanted to stand alongside every person before Christ, to put his arm around each one and say, "Father, this is Bill (or Mary, Joe, or Jack). I led him to faith in you. I taught him all the things you commanded. He has achieved full potential spiritually, and today, I present him to you complete."

I'm in full agreement with the Apostle Paul. When I stand before the Lord, I don't want to stand there alone, empty-handed. I want to bring someone with me who is fully grown and mature in Christ. In other words, I want to be a workman who needs not to be ashamed. The goal of every believer, as D. L. Moody said, should be " ... to go to heaven and to take as many people as possible with me."

Paul concludes by testifying, "Whereunto, I also labour, striving according to his working, which worketh in me mightily" (Colossians 1:29). The word "labour" means to toil, to grow weary, to exhaust oneself. "Strive," an athletic term, describes an athlete who exerts himself, pushes himself, and drives himself in training. In essence, Paul pushed and drove himself so that he might warn and teach every person, and ultimately present every person perfect in Jesus Christ.

Paul did this "according to his working, which worketh in me mightily." Translated from Greek, "working" means energy or power and here refers to the divine power of God. The idea is that, through faith in Christ, a person links his life with the source of energy that enables him to rise above his natural limitations. Two elements exist in Christian service—the human and the divine. Paul coupled himself with divine, the indwelling Christ, who energized him and kept him going.

Paul stated emphatically that his mission was to present to every person the fact that the indwelling Christ is the only hope of the world. And to that end, he drove himself. We should also labor and exert ourselves for this eternal cause as Paul did, so that spiritual laziness does not bring about our demise.

I read somewhere, that on the late President Lyndon Johnson's ranch house doormat, these words appear: "All the world is welcome here." Surely, if there are doormats outside the pearly gates, they will bear the same inscription. But "the world" will never know they are welcome unless we convince them to come in. This should be the consuming passion of our lives.

Paul set the precedent; and like him, we must spread the gospel, throughout our lifetime, to every person. Remember that Jesus said, " ... be thou faithful unto death, and I will give thee a crown of life" (Revelation 2:10). He did not say, "Be faithful until you are tired or retired"—but until you are expired. That is our challenge. Go forward!

3

Don't Sit There Until You Die

Church growth consultant, Phil Watson, once conducted a community survey and analysis for my former church, Green Acres Baptist Church of Tyler, Texas. He reviewed our record of achievement and identified extraordinary opportunity for our church: the potential for continued growth and greater impact on our city and county for Christ. In this regard, he said something I have never forgot: "Your church can choose to stop any place it decides. It is seldom an issue of potential but of attitude and vision that determines what people do."

No doubt, the statement lingered because it served to remind me that individuals and institutions alike can choose the path of life and growth. One of life's greatest tragedies occurs when someone dies at 30 and is buried at 60—much like the school teacher who applied for a new job. Her resume indicated 20 years of experience. But when the principal spied her old, yellow class notes, he called her former boss for a recommendation. He offered this assessment: "She doesn't have 20 years' experience. She has one year's experience 20 times." When a person ceases to grow, learn, dream, and progress, something inside him dies—regardless of his age.

Churches are no exception. Many of them stop far short of reaching their potential, then quickly decline because they lose their vision, faith and willingness to change. They become defenders of the status quo until they are impotent or die.

Such a church was established 40 years ago. Back then, this

country church lay some five miles out of the city limits. In time, the city surrounded the church, extending well beyond it. New homes, condominiums, apartments and businesses proliferated. Thousands of people moved within sight of the church, but the congregation simply sat there and did nothing. They remained a country church in thought and deed even though surrounded by the city. Those in control of the church dreamed small dreams, made small plans, and held little faith. They built no new buildings, inaugurated no new programs, called no new staff members, and made no effort to reach out to the many new people around them—so they remained small.

Sunday after Sunday, the church averaged 40 to 50 people in Sunday school, while other area churches grew at an explosive rate. The other churches gained new members from the area immediately surrounding the old rural church.

In time, the land on which the rural church was built became so valuable that the congregation sold out for a tidy sum, then moved to a new location adjacent to a thriving housing development. Once again this "rural" congregation sat and did nothing in spite of a new location and new facilities. Few new people were attracted because the old church clung to old attitudes and old practices. Gradually, the older church members died, and the younger members moved away. Finally, the old church could no longer afford to pay its pastor and was forced to close its doors. In the midst of growth and life, this church sat down and died.

That church's story is legion, having been repeated time and again. It speaks of a danger that confronts any and every church. Some churches must relocate or stagnate. But a mere change of location is not enough—it must be accompanied by a change in attitude. Churches can choose to stop at any time: however, if they choose to stop and do nothing, they die.

A story from the Bible vividly illustrates this situation. Ben Hadad, king of Syria, and his entire army, besieged the city of Samaria. Shortly thereafter, the city suffered a terrible famine; food was so scarce that people were eating animal refuse. An ass's head even sold for a much-inflated 80 pieces of silver. Some people resorted to cannibalism.

Although conditions were bad within the city, they were worse outside. The city gates kept out four starving lepers. Victims of dreadful disease and isolation, they pondered their fate: "Why sit we here until we die?" (2 Kings 7:3).

They assessed their situation, weighed their options and determined they had two choices: they could either sit outside the city gates and starve, or they could surrender to the enemy. If they surrendered to the Syrians, at worst they could be killed. Thus they reasoned, surrender might mean death; but remaining outside the gates meant certain death. Although surrender was risky, they had nothing to lose; the lepers took a chance.

On the way to surrender, they discovered God's deliverance. For the lepers, defeat became relief and victory when God caused the Syrian army to hear the approach of what seemed to be an immense army; the fearful Syrians immediately fled their camp. When the four lepers entered the camp, they discovered ample food. Because they acted, refused to "fossilize," and took a chance, the lepers' lives and eventually the populace, was saved.

Members of shrinking churches everywhere should ask themselves the question posed by the lepers. The answers will be the same: they could act and maybe die, or they could do nothing and surely die!

This is a certainty: churches cannot rest on their laurels. They cannot sit and do nothing, and expect to thrive. They must keep moving, thinking, growing, taking risks. In effect, churches must never stop starting, for if they do, the New Testament spirit will ultimately die inside them.

There are reasons churches sit and die, and alternate reasons they live and thrive.

Imaginative People Rule the World

First, churches sit and die because they lose their vision. The scriptures warn us, "Where there is no vision, the people perish..." (Proverbs 29:18). It is from our vision, our dreams, our imaginations that we receive a sense of mission. And a "mission" provides the essential fuel for a church. With no sense of mission, a church has no real reason to exist and cannot sustain an alive, exciting, vibrant fellowship. Whatever else a church does, it must never stop dreaming, planning, and progressing.

Dr. Victor Frankl, a noted Viennese psychiatrist, observed that failure to achieve our goals is less perilous than having no goals at all. He cited the Old Testament story of how God led the Hebrews through the wilderness, propelling them with a pillar of fire by night and a pillar of cloud by day.

Having goals means you never catch up with the cloud or the fire, and the "is" never touches the "ought." For the individual or a church to set a goal and reach it, but then not expand it, decay and death are inevitable. Quite simply, churches either develop from their dreams or decline toward an organizational death.

The goal of most churches, unfortunately, is to meet for an endless succession of "next Sundays." Beyond their Sundays lies no vision, no dreams, no sense of mission or doing something great for God.

Napoleon declared, "Men of imagination rule the world." The power of imagination, the ability to formulate mental images, is one of God's greatest gifts to man. When a man can conceive and believe, he can achieve. So it is that our imaginations provide inspiration for success: we must constantly imagine, dream dreams and visualize things we ought to do—then do them.

Thomas Jefferson expressed it aptly: "I like dreams of the future more than I like history of the past." In other words, where you are going is far more important than where you have been. Dreams are like stars; you may not touch them with your hands, but you need them to guide you through the darkness of the night.

Risk the Comfort Zone

Second, churches sit and die because they lack sufficient faith. Many churches are afraid to venture, to take a risk—even though accomplishment is within reach.

Churches are born out of a dream or out of a split. When a church emerges from a split, there is much to overcome. A positive, progressive spirit is difficult to build with a bunch of malcontents at the helm. On the other hand, when a church results from a dream of redemptive ministry, complacency can easily creep in, permitting decline from the very start. People can quickly become satisfied with the *status quo*; they no longer want to risk, to launch new ventures. They declare, "We have built enough. We have bought enough. We have borrowed enough. We are big enough." Such a risk-free attitude becomes an early warning sign of death in a congregation—no matter how the church started or what it may have accomplished.

Most people opt for the "comfort zone"—settling for security, rather than uncertainty—even if it means mediocrity and boredom. But take note: people are most insecure when their fears overtake their dreams.

Alfred Adler said, "The chief danger in life is: we take too many precautions." And Paul Tournier, in his book The Adventures of Living, reminds us that if life is not an adventure—full of risk and excitement—it is merely a dull, boring existence that hardly deserves to be called life. Certainly, this is true of "church life" as well as "private life."

One of the saddest episodes in Israel's history occurred at Kadesh Barnea. Only 18 months out of Egyptian bondage, the children of Israel arrived at the border of the Promised Land. There, Moses appointed "The Promised Land Search Committee." Their mission was to explore the land of Canaan and determine the way to "go up" (Numbers 13:17). Mind you, they were not empowered to determine "if" Israel were to go up, but "how" Israel would go up.

After 40 days, the committee of 12 spies returned with glowing reports on the land. It was all God had promised it would be and more: a land flowing with milk and honey (Numbers 13:27). No doubt, it was a land of opportunity, but there were also many obstacles which seemed insurmountable: well-fortified, walled cities and a population of giants (Numbers 14:32). The committee spokesman then described the situation: "And we were in our own sight as grasshoppers, and so were we in their sight" (Numbers 13:33).

Caleb, who did not agree with the majority report, immediately got the picture: the people were falling victim to fear, doubt, and disbelief. Aware that any good idea can be talked into oblivion, Caleb advised the children of Israel to take the land of milk and honey (Numbers 14:9).

Consumed with fear and doubt, the children of Israel refused to take the Promised Land and were then punished by the Lord for their lack of faith. They were forced to wander in the wilderness for 40 years. Ultimately, every person above the age of 20, save Caleb and Joshua, died without reaching the Promised Land.

Israel could have entered the Promised Land within 18 months; instead, they wandered the barren desert for four decades. Some churches have wandered the wilderness longer than 40 years—for the same reason. They lack the faith to believe God and the courage to act. So they sit and die.

Negative thinking is destructive. Those who see giants instead of God, will begin to think of themselves as grasshoppers and will soon act like grasshoppers.

Years later, David wrote of this same experience: "Yea, they turned back and tempted God, and limited the Holy One of Israel" (Psalms 78:41). How many churches today limit God by their lack of faith? The fact is, there were no giants (anakim) in the Promised Land when Joshua led the children of Israel there 40 years later. Either those giants never existed or they disappeared without a trace.

The Israelites were held back by their own internal weakness—a lack of faith—not the strength of the enemy. The giants were their own invention, merely illusions operating in their minds.

Perception and reality are not one and the same, but if we lack faith, they might as well be. God has set before many a church the Promised Land to be claimed—an incomparable opportunity. The condition is that a church have faith and the courage to risk.

A multitude of grasshopper Christians exists today, often led by grasshopper preachers. They see the obstacles far more often than the opportunities, the giants instead of God. Their motto is "Nothing ventured, nothing lost." They never travel a road unless they can first see the end. They never undertake a project unless the money is in hand. They never know the thrill of exploring with nothing but the assurance that God is leading them. God has never been able to accomplish anything with a coward, i.e., no Columbus ever discovered a new world reading books about adventure while hibernating at home.

Making progress means taking the plunge. Those who think they can do nothing, fulfill their expectations. They sever themselves from the source of strength. All successful Christian work is the work of God, accomplished through the faith of his people.

What we need is the commitment of a young William Carey — an Englishman of lowly position and uneducated even by the standards of his time—standing in the Nottingham Association with men of great repute. He offered them a proposition so far beyond their thoughts that they considered him insane. Yet, despite his ill treatment, he remained steadfast in preaching his message: "Expect great things from God. Attempt great things for God." Young Carey was a man of valor, not a grasshopper, and God honored his courage to bless the world.

Times Change

Third, churches sit and die because people refuse to change. They are inflexible, negative, and non-progressive.

I talked with a new pastor who spoke of a church building that had become an antique shop. I thought of several churches that function as little more than antique shops, although they still operated as churches. They are solely committed to old ways and outdated programs and steadfastly refuse to try anything new.

These are changing times. Times always have been changing. For instance, if you wanted to cross America in 1850, from east to west coast, you could have traveled by covered wagon in 166 days. Ten years later, the same journey by stagecoach would take 60 days. By 1870, you could travel westward by train for 11 days. In 1930, the same trip by air would take 26 1/2 hours. Today, in less than five hours, you can jet from east to west. And, if the space shuttle were an option, you could reduce the travel time from coast to coast to eight minutes. Just imagine! In less than 150 years, we have reduced travel time from 166 days to eight minutes!

When Henry Ford II, who was the grandson of Ford Motor

Company's founder, died, Automotive magazine called him "America's last great industrial Czar." It has been speculated that if Henry Ford II had not taken over the Ford Motor Company in 1945, there would be no Ford Motor Company today. At the time, the company was losing $1 million a day. His drive, determination, and energy turned the company around, restoring profitability and ushering it into another era.

Yet, those who knew him best felt that Henry Ford II remained as president of Ford too long. In the final years of his leadership, analysts indicated that he spent most of the time "trying not to make a mistake." The longer he stayed, the more backward the company became.

I was reminded of his grandfather, Henry Ford, founder of the company, and one of the greatest industrialists of all times. In 1903, he incorporated his Ford Motor Company. In 1908, he produced the Model-T Ford. In 1914, he paid his employees the unprecedented wage of five dollars a day so they could purchase his cars. He invented the assembly line.

Yet, in spite of his creative genius, Henry Ford possessed a fatal flaw. He developed an unhealthy fixation for his Model-T automobile. Although General Motors claimed an increasing share of the market at Ford's expense, old Henry refused to admit that the Model-T was passe'.

To maintain the Model-T's price at $290 (minus self-starter and removable rims), he continued to make the same car with the same archaic two-forward-speed planetary pedal transmission in a single color—solid black.

In the higher echelons of the company, Henry was surrounded by "yes-men," who never disagreed with him. Only his son, Edsel, and a few desperate sales managers were brave enough to tell him the Model-T had to go.

The elder Ford resisted, but confronted with declining sales figures, he finally gave in.

What happened to Henry Ford II as well as his grandfather, the founder of the company, can easily happen to any of us: we reach the point where we are more concerned about not making a mistake than we are with making progress. We develop such a fixation on what we have already done or what we are now doing that we become unwilling to consider alternatives or the possibility of change. In the end, we become caretakers, merely waiting for the undertakers!

A poet expressed it like this:
Our fathers have been churchmen,
for a hundred years or so,
And to every new proposal,
their answer always, is "No."

Churches need to realize that success is a moving target. What must a person or a church do to be successful? There is not any one thing you can do, but things you must keep doing. You are never safely there. The road to success is always under construction. Paul expressed it well: "I press toward the mark for the prize of the high calling of God in Christ Jesus"(Philippians 3:14).

A pastor friend of mine, whose church years ago needed a new building, shared his experience. He presented a proposal to the deacons, then opened the meeting for discussion.

One deacon, who always opposed everything, retorted, "I think I know our people, and I can speak for them. We need some relief from giving. We don't need this building."

Then a younger man spoke up: "I want to say two things. One, you don't speak for me or the church. You speak only for yourself. Two, if you and your group don't want to do anything, would you please shut up and let the rest of us go on?"

These are harsh words, but what the young deacon lacked in refinement, he made up in clarity and determination. We must go on or die. Change is inevitable, but progress is not. If we refuse to change with the times, we will be left behind. Will Rogers was right when he said, "Even if you are on the right track, you will get run over if you just sit there."

Martin Luther believed that "Our faith is a lively, reckless confidence in the grace of God." Indeed, there is no better way of neutralizing the fear of religious change than with such "a lively, reckless confidence" in the grace of God.

While visiting Australia several years ago, I saw a television advertisement promoting physical fitness. The ad featured an overweight man holding a can of beer, sitting in an easy chair "parked" in front of a television set. The narrator said, "Norm, get up. Turn the TV off. Go outside. Take a walk. Fly a kite. Do something. It's a matter of life and death."

What was happening physically to Norm happens to countless churches spiritually. If we sit and do nothing, we will also die—inwardly, spiritually. But, thank God, we don't have to. We can move forward with vision, faith and courage; and when we do, God blesses us with life and vitality. Go forward!

4

Plan For A Full House

During a television interview, Theodore White explained how, in 1964, Barry Goldwater won the Republican party presidential nomination over the better-financed Nelson Rockefeller. Goldwater won the nomination, said White, because he enlisted college students to solicit votes door-to-door. White concluded that, "The political battles of the future will be won on the doorsteps of America."

We can learn a lot about running churches from "the children of this world." If we are to win our world over to Christ, we must do it the same way: face-to-face, person-to-person, door-to-door.

Jesus emphasized this in the parable of the great supper. A man prepared a sumptuous feast and invited many people to dine with him (Luke 14:16-24). When the meal was ready, he sent his servants to those invited to tell them, "Come, for all things are now ready." But they all offered excuses for not attending.

When the servants informed their master, he became very angry. These people had all accepted his invitation, but now offered only empty, hollow excuses for their absence. He then commanded his servants to traverse the city streets and bring the poor, the maimed, the halt, and the blind to his supper.

When the servants returned from their second mission, they reported, "Lord, it is done as thou hast commanded, and yet there is room" (i.e., there were still empty seats).

The master then sent the servants on a third mission, this time into "the highways and the hedges" with the instruction, "Go ... and compel them to come in, that my house may be filled." The word "compel" in Greek is emphatic, meaning to necessitate or to urge. The master chose this word so that people who ordinarily would feel unwanted, unwelcome, and unworthy of attending would "fill his house."

The meaning of this parable is clear. The master represents God; the great supper represents salvation with all its blessings—the joy, the peace, the immense satisfaction and the privileges and responsibilities that accompany it. The servants represent you and me. As these servants were urgently sent out to invite people for the great supper, so we are to entreat people to share in salvation.

No people should be excluded; Gentiles and Jews, poor and rich, blacks and whites, the handicapped, the whole. Every race, every nationality, every color.

We are to go to them wherever they are: the streets and avenues of our cities, the country roads, high-rises or hovels. The message we are to deliver is a simple one: "All things are ready! Come."

Our message should be delivered with a sense of urgency. Everything is ready, and there is no time to spare. We must deliver our message repeatedly—until everyone, everywhere, knows they are wanted, welcome and worthy to sit at the Lord's table.

Many of our churches today seem to settle for less than our Lord would—a full house. Sadly, these churches are half empty, yet fully satisfied. Empty seats do not honor God. Vacant pews do not recommend him to an indifferent, preoccupied world. A full house, however, tells a different story. If God's people would show up, churches would fill up, and the world would sit up and take notice. The answer to packing the house, according to this parable, is to keep on going, again and again. Deliver the message heart-to-heart, person-to-person, door-to-door.

Our mission is clear. We must go with the conviction that all things are ready; all people are welcome; and all excuses are empty.

Public proclamation coupled with house-to-house visitation has been the commitment of my life. I became a Christian in my youth because a friend repeatedly asked me to attend Sunday school with him. Shortly after I committed to Christ, my church taught the book *Every Christian's Job* written by C. E. Matthews. From this study, I realized my responsibility to personally share my faith, and

I immediately began witnessing to others about Christ.

When the Lord called me to preach, I knew this was not merely a call to stand behind the pulpit publicly proclaiming the gospel. It was a summons to personal evangelism. That has been the basis for my ministry.

The first church I pastored was a small, country church that averaged about 40 members in Sunday school. The little community where the church was located had a grocery store, a cotton gin, a blacksmith shop, and a tavern. Cotton and corn farms dotted the countryside.

My wife and I would drive from Waco every Sunday morning for worship. Afterwards, we always joined one of the church families for lunch, and I would spend the afternoon visiting. No one really expected me to. No one told me to do it, but it was my compelling calling. I asked one of our deacons to sketch a map locating every farm house and identifying every family in the community. I then travelled each road and visited every house until I covered the entire community.

As a result of my visitation, within a year-and-a-half, our attendance in Sunday school climbed to 60 people, and we baptized more new converts than at any time in the church's recent history.

We had no baptistry in our own church, so we borrowed the baptistry from the Baptist church located six miles away in Troy. Before the year was over, we were using the baptistry more than they were. When the Troy church's pastor resigned, they called me as pastor.

Troy was a town of about 400 people. The church averaged 120 in Sunday school. There, I followed the same pattern I had established in Belfalls. I started at one end of a street and visited the first house; before I left, I identified the family next door, then visited them, and so on. Using this approach, in a short time, I visited and witnessed to every person in town. I then asked one of our deacons, who knew everyone in the countryside, to visit with me. Together, we travelled every country road in the area talking to people about Christ. Once again, God blessed our efforts with conversions and church growth.

After five years in Troy, I had completed my studies at Baylor

University and Southwestern Seminary. I then became pastor of the First Baptist Church in Taylor, a German and Bohemian farming town of 10,000 people in which the predominant churches were Lutheran, Roman Catholic, and Czech-Moravian Brethren. Baptists were a distinct minority; we averaged only 230 in Sunday school.

Once I had visited all my members and all the church prospects I knew of, I reverted to my tried and true methods. I started at the edge of town, went down the first street, and zigzagged back and forth, knocking on every door I encountered.

One day, I came to a house that was little more than a hovel. My first thought was that no one lived here, and I wouldn't bother to stop. Then I remembered my goal: to knock on every door in town.

I knocked on the door, and a shabbily dressed, elderly woman answered. She was not a Christian. I witnessed to her and asked if she would come to church. She replied that she would, but she did not have suitable clothes to wear. I asked one of the women in our congregation to help her with clothing, and the next Sunday the woman was in church. The following Sunday, she returned. The third week, I visited her a second time, and she accepted Christ as her Savior. As I was leaving, she said, "Pastor, I'll come forward next Sunday, and I want you to baptize me."

That was a Thursday night; on Saturday night, she died. Monday morning, I preached her funeral. Although this woman died, she died a Christian because of house-to-house visitation.

Not every visit bore fruit immediately. Down the same street, I visited a mother and her two teenage children, all of whom were totally indifferent to the gospel. Several weeks later, however, I received an urgent telephone call from the mother. She all but shouted, "There has been a serious automobile accident. We need you."

In a crisis situation, they needed a pastor. I was the only one the family knew, so she called me. As a result of ministering to the family through their crisis, the mother and her children became Christians. This family would never have been reached except through house-to-house visitation.

Five years later, I became pastor of the First Baptist Church of

San Marcos. The San Marcos population numbered 20,000, while the local state university added 11,000 students to the total. In my six years as pastor there, we averaged 100 baptisms per year. Most of these converts were won through personal evangelism. In San Marcos, as in the other places I had been, I continued evangelism during the week and preaching to Christians on Sunday.

Evangelism has never been a once-a-year, revival week spasm for me. It has, instead, been a day-to-day, week-by-week commitment. I believe the words of Roger Babson: "It is more essential to ring doorbells than church bells."

I challenge you to begin house-to-house, door-to-door visitations where you are. If you will, I guarantee results: people will be saved. Visitation is still the most effective means of filling God's house.

In light of my experience and the teaching of God's word, I offer some practical suggestions on the way to reach people and fill God's house.

Begin Among the People

First, do the work of an evangelist. That was Paul's advice to Timothy (2 Timothy 4:5). Paul did not advise Timothy to pitch a tent, print a brochure, and hold week-long revivals. "Evangelist" here means a bearer of good news. Paul instructed young Timothy that, as a pastor, he should always "do the work of an evangelist" by bringing the good news to people.

That is precisely my advice. Occasionally, a seminary student will ask me how to begin a new ministry. My advice remains steadfast: begin it among the people. Visit every member of your congregation in his home, then visit the lost of your community. Share the gospel with everyone.

The approaches many pastors want to take are to reorganize the Sunday school, "whip the deacons" into line, institute a purchase-order system, or rewrite the church constitution. My advice is not to tamper with the structure of the church until you have been there for some time and plan to stay. If you start too soon, you might not last as long as you had hoped.

There are solid reasons for following this advice. In the first place, people naturally resist change, and they will resist you. As management consultant Ray Bletze explained, "The only person who likes change is a wet baby."

Churches are, understandably, reluctant to change. Many small churches change pastors every 18 to 20 months, and every new pastor wants to make changes. And just about the time he changes everything and the members are thoroughly upset, he moves on. Then, in comes another pastor who starts the process over again. Little wonder that change is not always welcome.

Furthermore, change will accomplish little unless you stay a long time, for as soon as you leave, the church will revert to its old ways of operating. What's important to remember is that the Lord called us to change people, not to change structures.

Being a pastor-evangelist should be the top priority and a lifelong commitment of your ministry. Spend your time preaching, visiting, knowing your congregation, and winning souls. Pastors rarely encounter trouble when they follow these priorities.

Watch the Side Trips

Second, eliminate in order to concentrate. Early in my ministry, Cecil Sherman helped me understand this point. At that time, he served on the staff of the Evangelism Division of the Baptist General Convention of Texas, and was conducting an evangelism conference in the church I pastored. During his presentation, he asked our group, "What did you think God called you to do when he called you into the ministry?"

When there was no response, he directed the question to me. I responded with, "He called me to preach, to pray, and to visit."

Cecil offered a half-question, "That's right. So why don't you do that the rest of your life?" That meeting changed my life. Then and there, I became determined to concentrate on my ministry.

The problem most ministers face is not so much a crisis of time as a crisis of objectives. It is not that we don't do anything; it is that we often do too many things. The late Carlos McLeod teased, "The last year I pastored we could have observed 78 special weeks in our church!" Everyone and everything bids for our attendance, our attention, and our allegiance. As a minister, don't feel obligated to join every club, attend every meeting, or support every cause. If you aren't careful, the "many" things will separate you from the "main" thing.

A farmer once hitched his horse to a wagon for a trip to town. The old hound dog followed, running here and there chasing rabbits and anything else he could find. When the farmer arrived in town, his friend questioned the difference in the condition of the horse and that of the dog. Although the horse pulled the load, it seemed unaffected by the trip. But the panting hound dog appeared exhausted. The farmer explained: "It wasn't the trip that got the dog, it was all them side trips."

The same is true for us. We must decide what is most important and pare away all the "stuff" that clutters and confuses, steals our time and saps our strength.

Bloom Where You Are Planted

Third, deepen your ministry and let God broaden it. Don't spend your time making a name for yourself, climbing the ecclesiastical ladder, or looking for greener pastures. When I moved to Tyler and Green Acres, my boyhood pastor sent me a plaque that held excellent advice: "Bloom where you are planted."

If some ministers would spend half as much emotional energy building their own churches as they do locating a new church, they would already have a new church. It is our responsibility to deepen our ministry and God's responsibility to broaden it—if we do our part, he will certainly do his.

Concentrate on Output

Fourth, don't be weary in well doing. Set a goal to knock on every door in your neighborhood or town. Enlist your people to help, no matter how large or small the area. Determine how many evangelistic visits you can make per day, per week, per year. Establish a regular visitation time and, as often as possible, adhere to it. In other words, plan your work and work your plan.

Invest time in training your people. For instance, initiate a jail ministry and include your men for on-the-job training. Plan a deacon's retreat and teach them how to win people for Christ. Hold a series of weekly breakfasts for those who are interested in soul-winning to learn how to share their faith. Organize a Sunday night study course to teach people how to witness. Preach on evangelism often. Remember that your responsibility is not outcome, but output. If we are faithful, God will crown our efforts with success.

Know 9 Ways On How To Reach People

Don't rely on a single means of reaching people, but many ways. Here is a nine-point strategy for reaching people.

1. Collect information on newcomers from the utility companies as well as a newcomer service. Then visit each new person who moves to your community or city.

2. When people visit your services, welcome them warmly at announcement time. After you receive new members, invite visitors to a "Visitor's Reception" held in your study or other warm, inviting place immediately following the services. Many people will stay. Use these occasions to talk with them then about joining the church. You may even lead people to Christ as a result of this reception.

3. You, other staff members or volunteers should telephone each visitor on Sunday afternoon and invite them to attend services again. In phone conversations, we determine information vital to making visitation assignments. People are impressed when a church calls them so soon.

4. On Monday mornings, the names of newcomers and people who had visited the day before should be assigned to four different groups.

First, they are assigned to the staff (or pastor). Every member of the staff should visit a minimum of three prospects each week and report on these visits at a weekly staff meeting.

Second, they were assigned to a Sunday school class.

Third, they were assigned to a deacon. Consider dividing the deacon body into four visitation teams; each team devoting one Wednesday night per month to visitation.

Fourth, visitors are assigned to a member who lives nearby. Contact a member living in each visitor's neighborhood, encouraging them to call, offer a cake, or invite the visitor to their home for a get-acquainted meal.

You might ask, "With all that contact, might you ever overdo it?" The answer is "Yes." We once had a deacon visit the home of a doctor who had moved to town and attended our church the previous month. The deacon discovered this note attached to the door: "Please do not disturb. We plan to join Green Acres next Sunday." Sure enough, they did.

5. Try holding witness training one night each week. Those who participate often go door-to-door through apartment complexes and in designated neighborhoods.

6. Constantly encourage members to share their faith with others and invite people to attend your church.

7. Place visitors on your mailing list and send them your church paper for three months. Most people who move to a new community do not join a church immediately. During the first few months, they entertain out-of-town guests, make trips back home, and shop around for a church. Your church paper will serve as a weekly reminder that you are interested in them.

8. Once every quarter teach an "Inquirer's Class" on Sunday night before the worship hour. This class is intended primarily for people of other denominations who express interest in becoming members of your church. During the class, briefly review Baptist beliefs and the various ways someone can join your church. Get the name, address, and telephone number of each person attending the class. Then follow up with a phone call or visit.

9. Establish that each Wednesday night following prayer meeting will be your weekly visitation time, and seldom allow anything to interfere with this commitment. Every Christian worker needs to set a time for visitation. Without one, little visitation will occur. Pastors are not only the most effective visitors for the churches; they serve as an example for everyone else.

People soon recognize what you are and what is important to you. If you work hard—in other words, if you visit—they will know that. If you don't, they will also know that. Take prospects to lunch. Ask the church for an expense account just for this purpose. These lunch visits save you from much night work, but more importantly, give you an hour of uninterrupted time with the prospect—no ringing phones, no blaring televisions, no crying children. This can be one of the most effective outreach tools for a pastor.

When you leave town to attend a revival or meet a speaking engagement—even leave on vacation— always carry several prospect cards with you. Wherever you stay, purchase postcards to send personal notes to each of the prospects. It requires only minutes, but the recipients are greatly impressed that you would remember them while away. Sometimes call prospects long distance, an impressive gesture to a newcomer who feels lonely and forgotten.

Consider offering a pastor's Sunday school class in the auditorium each Sunday morning. Each spring and each fall, begin a new unit of study. Before introducing a new topic, direct a mailing to all people located in your ZIP Code area.

To many of you, this may seem like a lot of work. Or, you may not like my methods. That's okay. A lady once complained to D. L. Moody, "Mr. Moody, I don't like your methods." Moody reportedly replied, "Well, my dear, I don't care for some of them myself. What are yours?" She replied, "I don't have any." Moody then responded, "In that case, I like the way I am doing it better than the way you are not doing it."

The point is, if you don't like my methods, develop your own. Find a better way to fill God's house, then tell me about it. Go forward!

5

Utilize The Body

In spite of media attacks, stereotypes or neglect of the Church—fueled by the indiscretions of a few ministers—I remain "bullish" on the Church and churches. They are the only movement Jesus left on earth to do his work.

Many other causes deserve our support and interest, but if you want to be on the cutting edge of the kingdom of God, you need to be vitally involved in a local church. As far as God is concerned, that's where the action is.

The role of the church is greatly misunderstood today, for many people view it as they would a civic club. To them, the church is an organization to join, attend meetings, pay dues, and perhaps enjoy the fellowship and any status associated with belonging. But the Bible presents an entirely different picture—several pictures in fact—of the church. Sometimes the church is called "the bride of Christ," and other times "the building of God." Most often, it is called "the body of Christ."

A bride is the woman a man chooses as his wife, the one to whom he commits himself for life. A building is a structure in which a person dwells, and a body is the means through which a person reveals his personality and through which he acts. The church, then, is the people of God to whom Christ is committed, in whom Christ dwells, and through whom Christ works.

The Church as the Body of Christ

Paul uses this analogy 15 times in his letters. In Ephesians

(1:22-23) for instance, he writes that God has put all things under Christ's feet and appointed him as head over all things to the church, "which is his body..." Precisely what do the scriptures mean when they refer to the church as the body of Christ?

For 33 years, Jesus incarnated himself in a human body. Through that body, he went about doing good. In time, he died on the cross, was buried, rose from the dead, and ascended into heaven. On the Day of Pentecost, the living spirit of Christ, the Holy Spirit, came to dwell in his people and to constitute his church. Although he was incarnated in a body for 33 years, he now perpetually incarnates himself in his new body: the church.

We are now his body on earth, meaning that, in part, we are the means through which he expresses his personality and through which he acts. The world does not see Christ unless it sees him in and through us. We are the blood and bone and muscle by which he walks in the marketplace.

The Bible declares Jesus to be the head of the church. This means that the church shares the same relationship to Christ as my body does to my head. The church, therefore, is not merely an institution or an organization; it is an organism. It has a living, vital, dynamic relationship with Christ. And because Christ lives in us and works through us, he is able to do his work in the world.

My head is the control center of my life, where my thinking takes place. It is the seat of my will, the root of my decisions. My body will not act unless, first, my mind tells it to do so. If I reach out with my hand, it is because my mind shoots an impulse through my nerves and muscles, telling it to respond. If I take a step, it is because my mind directs my feet to move. If I speak, my mind makes that decision first, relaying the message on to my vocal cords. My head makes the decisions; my body simply carries them out.

In the same manner, Jesus Christ directs and dictates the actions of the church. The church carries out his will, obeys his commands, and performs his work on earth. Often, a person's mind can be sharp and clear, functioning normally, while his body remains incapacitated. This functional loss, or dysfunction, assumes several forms: paralysis as the result of an accident, waste due to disease, or weakness caused by inactivity and age.

In a similar manner, the body of Christ experiences paralysis, the victim of fear or indifference rather than accident. It wastes away, ravaged by strife and inactivity, as deadly as any disease. Or it grows debilitated, old in its vision and spirit.

Unfortunately, the local church body of Christ often is not as healthy and vigorous as it should be. Christ, the head of the church, is very much alive and well, but his body lags behind, weak and anemic. As the body of Christ, what can we do to restore its vitality? What is our responsibility, our mission on earth? We need only to look at Jesus and what he did through his earthly body for the answers. That is what we should do as his body today.

So, what did Jesus do? He fed the hungry, clothed the naked, healed the sick, befriended sinners, preached the gospel, and eventually gave his own life for the world. He enlisted his body in the service of humanity—seeing, listening, loving, touching, feeling, healing, and preaching.

Successful ministers are servants, not spectators in the arena of life. We are the hands of Christ reaching out to the needy, the eyes of Christ detecting hurt in human hearts, the ears of Christ attending to cries of distress, the feet of Christ rushing to those in need, and the voice of Christ carrying the message of hope, salvation and eternal life. We are all part of the body of Christ, and we must function accordingly.

In practical terms, then, what is the church? It is a mind through which Christ thinks; a heart through which Christ loves; a hand through which Christ helps; and a voice through which Christ speaks.

A Lesson From Herschel Walker

The church is a mind through which Christ thinks. At the close of the 1986 football year, Texas newspapers reported that former Dallas Cowboy running back Herschel Walker might end his NFL career after that season. Sportswriters carried his comment into the headlines—"Walker: 'I might retire.'"

Team president Tex Schramm expressed little concern, confident that Walker was not issuing a threat. Schramm added that "He is a lot like Tom Landry. He's a Christian-thinking kind of person. He believes that he will do what the Lord has planned for him."

In calling Walker "a Christian-thinking kind of person," Schramm acknowledged that Christ did not think like the rest of the world. If we are his body on earth today, we should think differently, for we are a mind through which Christ thinks. We must, therefore, not defend the status quo or echo the philosophies of life expressed around us. Instead, we must think as Christ thinks and reflect him.

The world thinks, "You've got to find yourself." But Jesus said, "For whosoever will save his life shall lose it; but whosoever shall lose his life for my sake and the gospel's, the same shall save it" (Mark 8:35). It seems that we are forever trying to "find ourselves," when we really need to lose our "self."

The world thinks it's every man for himself. But Christ thinks, "Greater love hath no man than this, that a man lay down his life for his friend" (John 15:13).

The world thinks you need to get all you can, can all you get, and sit on the lid. But Jesus thinks a person's life consists of more than the abundance of the things possessed.

The world thinks you only go around once in life, so grab for all you can get. Our Lord asks, however, "For what is a man profited, if he shall gain the whole world, and lose his own soul?" (Matthew 16:26).

The world thinks if it feels good, do it. Scripture tells us, "Be not deceived; God is not mocked: for whatsoever a man soweth, that shall he also reap" (Galatians 6:7).

The world thinks you need to go along to get along. But God says through Paul, "And be not conformed to this world: but be ye transformed..." (Romans 12:2).

We must never stoop to the world's level of thinking, for the church is a mind through which Christ thinks. Some people feel that the church should reflect the spirit of the age. Nonsense! As the Rock of Ages, the church should speak the ageless truth of God to our own perishing age. When the church identifies itself with the world, materialism and worldliness gain a foothold. It becomes little more than a glorified social club.

Listen as the scriptures direct our thinking: "Let this mind be in you, which was also in Christ Jesus..." (Philippians 2:5).   And, "Finally, brethren, whatsoever things are true, whatsoever things are honest, whatsoever things are just, whatsoever things are pure, whatsoever things are lovely, whatsoever things are of good report; if there be any virtue, and if there be any praise, think on these things" (Philippians 4:8).

I Want Attention

Second, the church is a heart through which Christ loves. When I was a pastor, I closed each Sunday evening worship service by inviting all children to gather in the front of the sanctuary; there, we sat on the steps, and I talked with those who had birthdays that week. I would ask them to describe their favorite gift. One night, a young girl came forward to tell me about her birthday which was two days away. I asked her what she wanted for her birthday. After a long silence, she said, "I'd like a little attention."

"From anybody in particular?" I asked.

"Yes, from my brother," she replied.

In truth, many people wish for a little attention in life. As his body, we are to love them and give it to them.

Jesus paid attention to everyone. He loved little children and big sinners. He loved loose women and rigid Pharisees, rich young rulers and poor old beggars. Regardless of persons' upbringings or downfalls, he loved them all. So should we, for we are the heart through which he loves.

Remember the bumper sticker that read "Honk if you love Jesus"? Perhaps you also remember one that said: "If you love Jesus, tithe. Anyone can honk."

Some people are nothing more than "spiritual honkers," going through life tooting instead of tithing and telling. They give no concrete evidence of their love.

Bishop William Lawrence observed that the great American heresy is to think that because a thing has been said, it has been done. We Christians must be careful not to substitute words for deeds. Words are useful in defining, explaining, and illustrating our actions, but are no substitution for deeds. As the Apostle John would have us remember, "My little children, let us love not in word, neither in tongue, but in deed and in truth."

Look at Your Hands

Third, the church is a hand through which Christ helps. In the courtyard of a quaint little church in a French village there stood a beautiful statue of Jesus with his hands outstretched.

One day during World War II, a bomb struck too close to the statue, and it was dismembered. After the battle was over, the citizens of the village patiently gathered the broken pieces of their beloved statue, then reassembled it. Although the scars on the body added to its mystical beauty, one problem remained: the hands were nowhere to be found. "A Christ without hands is no Christ at all," one citizen lamented. "Hands with scars, yes. But what's a Lord without hands? We need a new statue." Another citizen offered the best solution. A bronze plaque was affixed to the base of the statue, which read: "I have no hands but your hands."

Years later, a poet—identity unknown— saw the inscription and wrote these lines:

Christ has no hands but our hands
To do his work today;
He has no feet but our feet
To lead men in his way.
He has no tongues but our tongues,
To tell men how He died.
He has no help but our help,
To bring them to his side.
We are the only Bible
The careless world will read.
We are the sinner's gospel,
We are the scoffer's creed;
We are the Lord's last message
Written in deed and word—
What if the line be crooked?
What if the type be blurred. (Schuller, p. 103)

Years ago, Alexander Irvine wrote a novel called My Lady of the Chimney Corner. In one incident, "the lady" comforts a neighbor whose son lay dead.

"Ah, woman, God isn't a printed book to be carried around by a man in fine clothes ... nor a gold cross to be danglin' at the watch chain of a priest. God's Spirit comes in as many ways as there's need for it coming ... God takes a hand wherever He can find it, and just does what He likes with it. Sometimes He takes a Bishop's hand and lays it on a child's head in benediction, then He takes the hand of a doctor to relieve pain, the hand of a mother to guide a child, and sometimes He takes the hand of a poor old critter like me to give comfort to a neighbor. But they're all hands touched by His spirit, and His spirit is everywhere lurkin' for hands to use."

Our prayer should be, "Oh, God, won't you use my hands?" The answer to meeting the needs of the world is not just to add more staff members to the church, but for us all to serve as the hands of Christ.

My last congregation had more than 7,000 members. If each member had given one hour of volunteer work per week, the equivalent would have been 175 full-time employees. Consider how many hungry could have been fed, how many lonely could have been visited, how many lost could have been won if we had 175 more full-time Christian workers!

In *Jesus, The Word to Be Spoken,* Mother Teresa observed that every Christian should ask himself three questions: "You need only to ask at night before you go to bed, 'What did I do to Jesus today? What did I do for Jesus today? What did I do with Jesus today?' You have only to look at your hands. This is the best examination of conscience."

Too often, Christians view the church as a sanctuary, a retreat from an evil world. And far too often, Christians hide behind stained-glass windows, muffling the cries of an anguished world with blaring music. As Christians, we should stop blaming God for being absent when we are absent ourselves. After all, we are his body, his hands. We must get back in touch with the world to do his work.

Soup, Soap, Salvation

Fourth, the church is a voice through which Christ speaks. The church belongs to God, not to man, and therefore, cannot become a tool of the social order. People are hungry, naked, sick, ignorant, and in need of our help. But, first and foremost, people are lost and need to be saved.

If we do not feed the hungry, clothe the naked, or minister to the sick, perhaps others may step in. But if our voices are silent, who will tell them the Good News? If the church does not proclaim, "Jesus saves," who will?

"Soup! Soap! And Salvation!" served as the motto for the Salvation Army and its colorful director, William Booth, for many years. General Booth believed that the Salvation Army's mission should be to "Clean them up! Fill them up! Lift them up!" As the body of Christ, our mission is much the same: clean people up, fill people up, but most important, lift people up so they can be saved.

There is a legend concerning a saint about to make the journey from Rome to Jerusalem. The night before he left, he dreamed of a beggar sitting at the gates of Rome, pitiful and clad only in rags. A voice from the dream spoke to the saint: "Do you see that man? That is the Messiah, dressed as a beggar." The saint awoke, but could not escape the disturbing dream. Throughout his pilgrimage, he was reminded of the dream. Toward the end of his journey, as he approached the gates of Jerusalem, a disheveled figure dressed in rags sat precisely as in the dream. The saint inquired of him: "Is it true that you are the Messiah?" The beggar nodded.

The saint then asked, "What are you doing here at the gates of Jerusalem?"

The man answered, "Waiting."

"Waiting in a world full of misery and hatred and war? In a world where God's people are scattered and oppressed? In a world where children go hungry, and you sit here waiting? Messiah, in the name of God, what are you waiting for?" queried the saint.

Said the Messiah, "I've been waiting for you so I could ask you, in the name of God, what are you waiting for?"

If we are, indeed, a voice through which Christ speaks, what are we waiting for?

6

Lead By Persuasion

As I travel about the country talking with pastors and church leaders, I discover them struggling most with the question of authority and leadership in the church. This is, I believe, one of the most pressing issues facing our churches today.

Our churches are either trying to resolve the question of who is the leader, or they are trying to deal with the problems and mistakes of leadership. A major reason this is such a crucial matter is that no church can grow to its highest potential and reach the lost unless there is good leadership. And there can be no good leadership unless there is a good relationship between a pastor and staff people. And basic to a good relationship is the right understanding of leadership in the church.

One of the key passages of Scripture that speaks to this subject is found in the Book of Hebrews.

"Remember them which have the rule over you, who have spoken unto you the Word of God: whose faith follow, considering the end of their conversation [lifestyle, manner of living, walk]. Obey them that have the rule over you, and submit yourselves: for they watch for your souls, as they that must give account, that they may do it with joy, and not with grief: for that is unprofitable for you" (Heb. 13:7, 17).

At first reading, these verses seem to suggest the pastor has absolute authority in the church—that he is in control—he is the potentate, and the people are to obey him and submit to him. There are three words in particular within these verses that seem to suggest this: They are the word "rule" (used twice), the word "obey," and the word "submit." However, a careful examination of these verses in the original language gives a vastly different picture. The Greek word translated "rule" employed here means "to lead." Herschel Hobbs writes of this word, "It is best translated 'the one who is in front of you.'" [Baptist Beliefs: Baptist Standard, July 27, 1988, p. 7.] The "Criswell Study Bible" points out that this is not the word which is generally used to mean "to reign" as king or governor. There is such a word for that in the Greek language, but the Holy Spirit did not choose to employ that word here. [The Criswell Study Bible. Thomas Nelson Publishers, Nashville; 1979, p. 1443, footnote on Heb. 3:7.]

The word "obey" is most often translated "to persuade, to convince." It is from the same root word used by King Agrippa when he admitted to the apostle Paul, "Almost thou persuadest me to be a Christian" (Acts 26:28).

The word "submit" means "to yield." These two words together mean that we are to remain persuadable and pliable to the teachings and leadership of those whom God has called to look after our spiritual welfare. We are to keep a responsive heart, an open mind, and a teachable spirit toward God's ministers. We are not to be "stiff-necked" as was Israel of old.

So, the best interpretation of these verses from Hebrews is not that the pastor is to be a dictator, but that he is one who leads by persuasion—"friendly persuasion." He does not command the church; he rather should attempt to convince the church. And the church should be open and receptive to God's truth as the pastor presents it. The church should be willing to be persuaded and to yield to the truth when it is presented.

If you have any doubts about this, read Peter's advice to pastors. He advised that they should go about their sacred duties "not as lords over God's heritage, but being examples to the flock" (1 Pet. 5:3). Remember that the Scriptures always harmonize and are never contradictory. The pastor is not to be a dictator. He is to lead by spiritual example, by influence, by persuasion. He is to persuade his people by the life he lives, the example he sets, and the truth he preaches.

Pay attention to several facts from this Hebrews passage:

First, notice the realm of pastoral leadership. The writer refers here to spiritual leadership, not church administration. He is not talking about the pastor leading the church to buy property or to construct a building, for the early church had neither of these. He has in mind the pastor's preaching and teaching . . . his instruction and spiritual guidance that should be followed. Members should be open and responsive to him as he preaches God's Word to us, for a God-called pastor will, in word and deed, care for our souls.

Second, notice the responsibility of leadership. The leader is one who "must give account." I heard a pastor give an unusual interpretation of this statement. He quipped that long after most Christians are enjoying heaven, their pastors will still be standing outside the pearly gates. "Having given an account for himself, he is then going to have to give an account for every one of us" (i.e., all his members)! When I heard him make that half-facetious remark, my first thought was, If that's true, I'm going to get out of this job right now. It will be hard enough to give an account for myself. I'm not about to try to answer for everyone in my congregation!

That, of course, is not what the writer of Hebrews meant at all. He was emphasizing that pastors must give an account for how they have taught, what they have preached, and the manner in which they have led their people. They are responsible to God not only for their own lives but also for the leadership they give to the Lord's church. They will answer to Him at the judgment seat of Christ. That is an awesome responsibility.

Third, notice the response the church should make to leadership. Church members should listen to and learn from the pastor so his ministry will not be "unprofitable" for them. In Ephesians, Paul points out that the Lord provides gifted leaders to the church to equip us for service and edify us (build us up) spiritually (Ephesians 4:11-12). If we do not honor and respect our Christian leaders, if we are not responsive as they preach and teach the truth, if we turn a deaf ear to them, the Lord will be unable to accomplish His own mission through us.

When Peter the Great, Czar of Russia, assumed power more than three centuries ago, he vowed to modernize Russia and deliver it from the "dark ages." Czar Peter learned all he could from other countries by travelling incognito throughout Europe. Upon his return to Russia, he swore to "take Russia into modern times if I have to drag her kicking and screaming."

Nowhere in the New Testament does the pastor appear as a ruler; his role is purely leadership and inspiration. Unlike Czar Peter, when a pastor has to drag his people forward kicking and screaming, the ministry becomes a burden to him and unprofitable for them.

Speaking on the subject of pastoral leadership at a conference, I said, "It's the pastor's responsibility to lead and to feed his people." One of the pastors in the audience responded with, "Yeah, and it's the people's responsibility to follow and swallow!"

That gave us all a moment of laughter, but it is not scriptural. The biblical pattern was explained by the Apostle Paul writing about the people at Berea: "These were more noble than those in Thessalonica, in that they received the word with all readiness of mind, and searched the scriptures daily, whether those things were so" (Acts 17:11).

Dictators, whether political or ecclesiastical, suffer from insecurity. They cannot tolerate dissent or diversity of opinion, so they get rid of the opposition. Only strong, secure, and confident leaders allow opposition without suppression.

The apostles in the early church were awarded special authority by the Lord, although they seldom used it. They chose, rather, to lead by persuasion. In the sixth chapter of Acts, a dispute over aid to widows arose in the Jerusalem church. The Greeks felt neglected and complained. Although the apostles were handling the matter, it consumed so much of their time that their spiritual ministries suffered. The apostles proposed a viable solution allowing others to effectively take over this task: "Look ye out among you seven men of honest report, full of the Holy Ghost and wisdom, whom we may appoint over this business...And the saying pleased the whole multitude: and they chose..." (Acts 6:3).

A clear pattern emerges here. When a problem arose, the apostles proposed the solution and persuaded the church it was the right path. The "whole" church acted, and the work of God moved forward with renewed vigor.

A similar pattern emerged at the Jerusalem Conference, where the church was angered over the doctrine of salvation. The Judaizers argued, "Except you be circumcised after the manner of Moses you cannot be saved" (Acts 15:1). They were opposed by those who viewed salvation as attainable by grace through faith in Christ alone. Debate and argument resulted in what the Bible calls "no small dissension and disputation" (Acts 15:2).

Under the leadership of Paul, Barnabas and the other apostles, the issue was settled: salvation by grace through faith prevailed. Persuasion, once again, proved to be the key: "then pleased it the apostles and elders, with the whole church..." (Acts 15:22).

When the church found itself having to deal with a brother living in immorality, Paul passively advised they should dismiss him from the fellowship "when ye are gathered together" (1 Corinthians 5). Hence, the church was called together, it acted in the name and through the power of the Lord Jesus Christ.

Paul also urged—not ordered—the church to gather an offering for the relief of the Jerusalem saints. Paul promoted his request by "allowing" the church to choose the messengers: "whomsoever you shall approve by your letters [of recommendation], them will I send to bring the offering to Jerusalem" (1 Corinthians 16:2-4).

The Epistle of Philemon contains yet another persuasive example. Onesimus, Philemon's slave, fled from Colosse to Rome, where Paul led him to Christ. Onesimus returned home bearing a letter from Paul asking Philemon to receive Onesimus as a Christian brother, not a slave. As an Apostle, Paul could have demanded Philemon's cooperation; instead, he wrote one of the most diplomatic appeals on record. The decision was left entirely to Philemon.

This was clearly the pattern set forth in the New Testament: leadership by persuasion, influence, example rather than orders, edicts or ecclesiastical decrees. A wise pastor will follow the New Testament pattern, involving his people in devising a program and then work harder than anyone to fulfill it.

One of the most difficult tasks in the world, leading by persuasion, calls for the wisdom of Solomon, the patience of Job, and the strength of Samson. You constantly walk an emotional tightrope, for as a minister, your helpers are most often volunteers—people who cannot be commanded, but are often ready to criticize, or those who are eager to start work but fail to finish the job. As a leader, you may fail, or make mistakes in personal judgment. In the ministry, there are always enough successes to keep you on your feet and enough failures to keep you on your knees.

So, a minister should lead by persuasion.

What are the some marks of a true Christian leader?

Be A Servant

First, he is trusted by his people. It is amazing what people will do for you if they trust and believe in you; and they will trust you if they believe you have their best interests at heart. If you wish to lead by persuasion, you must lead from the perspective of servant. According to Hebrews (13:17), leaders "watch for your souls"; without a doubt, people will follow, if they believe you care for their souls.

Take the Initiative

Second, he takes the initiative. A genuine leader never waits for others to propose and take action; he acts and moves toward achievement, regardless of his rank or station.

To be successful as a leader, you must accept and practice these principles: identify the need; devise a solution; convince others that you are correct and enlist their help to support the plan; delegate responsibility by inspiring others to join you; and work alongside others to achieve the goal.

Don't Gamble

Third, he uses good judgement. When something really counts, a leader doesn't gamble; he may take a calculated risk, but never trusts luck. And, he avoids stupid mistakes. Pastors are not allowed many mistakes without sacrificing people's confidence. Often a minister who fails does so because of poor judgment and lack of common sense—not because of his preaching or morals or lack of visitation.

Years ago, on the radio show "Amos 'n' Andy," Amos one day asked the Kingfish why he had such good judgment. "Well", replied the Kingfish, "good judgment comes from experience."

"Then where does experience come from?" asked Amos.

"From bad judgment," admitted the Kingfish.

Good leaders learn from their own mistakes and the mistakes of others.

Speak With Confidence

Fourth, a good leader speaks with authority. He knows his subject, speaks authoritatively from the pulpit, but stops short of being brash. Jesus was known as "one who has authority." He knew his subject and meant what he said. Sensing his authority, people followed him. People are searching for authority today just as they were during Jesus's time; if, as a pastor, you command authority and respect, people will follow.

Get Excited

Fifth, he is enthusiastic. And enthusiasm does not emanate from the cheerleader spirit but the holy spirit. Enthusiasm is derived from the words en and theos meaning "God in us." Therefore, energy, excitement and expectation combine to make the Christian leadership spirit one that is a joyful, meaningful, and easy to follow.

Look for Opportunities

Sixth, a leader is optimistic. There is an old saying that "A pessimist sees difficulty in every opportunity, and an optimist sees an opportunity in every difficulty." Good leaders focus on objectives, not obstacles. Like good hurdlers, they focus on the finish line, not the hurdle. They see the destination, not impediments that block the way. Against the odds, in the face of opposition, optimistic spirits never flag—and good leaders win.

Set the Pace

Seventh, he leads by example. Like the apostle Paul, a good leader establishes a pattern for others to follow. Paul challenged his readers to follow him just as he followed Christ. Paul also challenged

Timothy to exemplify the believer and instructed the elders to serve as examples to the flock.

The Bible advises older women to be models for younger women (Titus 2:3-5). In Hebrews, the writer tells believers to "remember your leaders, who speak the word of God to you. Consider the outcome of their way of life and imitate their faith" (Hebrews 13:7).

Motivate the People

Eighth, he activates others. A good leader delegates to others and gets them involved, helping them grow and increase their productivity. Moses learned this from his father-in-law (Exodus 18:1-27) just as you must learn this from Jesus Christ.

The writer of Hebrews tells us that "Jesus Christ is the same yesterday, today and forever." In others words, his preeminence is permanent, his leadership everlasting. Although we will eventually pass from the scene, Christ is eternal. And therein lies the secret of earthly leadership: to be led by Jesus Christ, for all ages unchanging. Those who lead the church to greatness are themselves led by Christ.

7

Make A Great Commotion About The Great Commission

"A church that is not missionary," preached George W. Truett, "does not deserve the ground upon which its buildings stand." Unfortunately, with regard to many churches, when all has been said and done about missions, more has been said than done. We pay lip service to the Master's missionary mandate.

In my pastorates, we attempted to be missionary not in words only, but in deed and in truth as well. To this end, we were committed to both cooperative and direct missions, local and foreign missions, social ministries, and church planting. In short, we tried to do it all. The main reason for including a chapter on missions is to encourage you and your church to become involved n much-needed missionary work. A truly evangelistic church demands it.

This chapter is very much biographical; not my biography but the missions biography of Green Acres Baptist Church in Tyler, Texas. It is dedicated to those remarkable people who answered a call to missions and did whatever was necessary to fulfill that call.

That primary commitment was aimed at cooperative missions through our denomination. Liberal giving through cooperative means sets free the missionaries to devote their full energies to missionary work. This is an opportunity for every church—from the smallest to the largest—to participate in fulfilling the Great Commission.

In addition to cooperative missions, Green Acres Church created direct missions. For more than a decade, we built one church per year in a foreign country—two in Brazil, two in Mexico, eight in Belize, Central America. Locally, the church sponsored eight missions—one Korean, two Hispanic, one African-American, and four predominantly Anglo. Future plans for overseas and local mission sponsorship are ambitious, especially in the development of local missions designed to reach lower income groups with no neighborhood church.

Accident or Providence?

Green Acres became involved with direct missions almost by accident—or perhaps "by providence." Years ago, the missions committee learned that the tiny border town of Diaz Ordaz, Mexico, needed a church. Diaz Ordaz was best known as a center of border drug trade. The First Baptist Church of Reynosa planned to serve as the sponsoring church if we would erect the building. Our church, like most, however, never seemed to have excess funds, and we had no idea how to raise the necessary $20,000 for the building.

Our missions committee offered a solution: that we double our Christmas offering for foreign missions to $40,000 that year. That way, half the money would be designated for foreign missions through our denomination; the other half would be used to build the church in Mexico. For the first time, Green Acres reached its Christmas missions goal before the end of December. The reason? Building a church became a personal issue for our congregation. With the two mission efforts tied together, the entire program goal was enhanced—and each year since, Green Acres has added the cost of building a church in a foreign country to its Christmas mission offering with resounding success.

Bibles and Buildings for Belize

Belize, one of the poorest countries in Central America, became the church's direct mission focus. Once a colony of Great Britain, Belize was known as British Honduras before England granted its independence.

I became acquainted with Belize in the early 1970s by accompanying Dr. Kerfoot Walker, a physician and deacon in the church, on one of his many Central American treks to provide the population with medical assistance under the auspices of Amigos International. This trip became one of many for me, working closely with Dr. Walker and later with Baptist missionary couples who had been eventually assigned to Belize.

On one occasion, missionary Otis Brady asked me to preach in each of the five existing churches in an effort to "call out the called." He and others had been praying earnestly that God would call Belizian nationals into the ministry, preparing them to lead their own churches. In four days of preaching, 14 young men surrendered their lives to the ministry!

Some time later, Phil Hook, a former seminary professor, now a member or our church, travelled to Belize to help in the training of these young ministers. Upon his return, he urged us to concentrate on evangelizing the entire country. I prayed for a strategy, ultimately concluding that we should devote our efforts to evangelizing Belize for the next five years. In communicating this to our missionary leadership in Richmond, Virginia, we said that we would work for them but only at their specific request. We would build as many church buildings as they requested, place a Bible in the hand of every Belizian, and send teams to organize vacation Bible schools, revivals, and leadership training.

In that eight years, Green Acres Church built a retreat center, trained many national leaders, saw eight churches erected and thousands of people saved. While dedicating a building we had built, one of the laymen in the congregation testified that he and his wife had prayed for 14 years that a church would locate in their community. Prayers were answered that day!

God performed miracles in the lives of Green Acres people, as well as those in Belize, because of missions involvement. One of these people, "Pee Wee" Edmonds, participated in a Belize missions trip, helping to construct a church by day and distributing Bibles door-to-door in the evenings. The product of a broken home and "on his own" since the age of 14, Pee Wee responded to the gospel for the first time on that trip. He accepted Christ and was baptized in the Caribbean Sea. Pee Wee and his family are now active members of Green Acres and strong supporters of missions.

The close association of the Green Acres people with Southern Baptist missionaries and their direct involvement in church planting has produced a commitment to missions that is truly remarkable. By combining direct missions with our cooperative effort, we greatly enhanced both.

Where God Guides, He Provides

Locally, missionary involvement has been fully as exciting. Several years ago, I felt an impression from the Lord that our church should become more involved in local mission work. I am not a mystical person, so I never heard a voice or saw a vision. I simply had an inner feeling that this was what God wanted us to do. Outside of his written word, this is the only way God has ever spoken to me.

When the time was right, I asked our church to make a one-year pledge to pay off our building debt. We would then use the $12,000 monthly interest we saved to perform local mission work. While we were in the process of promoting our pledge day, three mission opportunities appeared.

A Korean pastor from Houston called to say that a number of Korean families lived in Tyler. He wished to begin mission work among them and wondered if our church would sponsor it. I told him that we would, and in less than five minutes, we were sponsors of a Korean mission.

Some weeks later, our local Baptist association requested that we assume sponsorship of an existing Hispanic mission, one that lacked strong leadership and supervision. Once again, we accepted the challenge and our second mission opportunity.

Not long after that, our third opportunity arrived. The pastor of a struggling Anglo church, Sylvania Baptist, asked that we adopt them as a mission. At one time a strong congregation, Sylvania Baptist had since suffered the loss of young members and its leaders, leaving them helpless without sponsorship. We welcomed mission number three.

By the time pledge day arrived, we had accepted the challenge and responsibility of mission sponsorship three times. Out of this, we saw emerge a spiritual principle that every church needs to know. Where God guides, he provides. We often do nothing because we don't see the opportunity. Or, we feel that our resources are not strong enough to meet the obligation. God provided for both as the people committed to the ministry.

Now, For the Rest of the Story

As Paul Harvey says, "and now for the rest of the story." The story gets even better. On pledge day, a visitor from Dallas attended the worship service and stayed for the visitor's fellowship which directly followed. At his invitation, he and I enjoyed lunch together later in the week. At that time, he mentioned that his secretary's husband served as assistant director of missions for a large Dallas church. He then issued an amazing offer: "I don't know if you are interested in local missions, but if you are, and if you like this man, I will give you $25,000 a year for the next five years to pay his salary."

In addition, he wanted to contribute $12,000 to our church for local mission work. There—it had happened again. Where God guided, he provided.

When this mission assistant was settled and on the field, he suggested that we build a mobile dental/medical clinic to meet the needs of disadvantaged people in our community. As we would move the unit around the area, we would share the gospel with them; these initial preaching points would eventually become churches. One day, over lunch, I shared the dream with Bruce Brookshire a Presbyterian layman. Before we departed, he handed me a check to cover the mobile clinic in full. Again—where God guided, he provided.

Within the year, we caught a vision for an outreach center in north Tyler. It would be a place to feed the hungry, clothe the poor, and house the homeless. After several disappointing weeks of searching, we located a disbanded church facility, just the right size and located in the center of Tyler's disadvantaged. Although the FSLIC (who had taken the property over from a defunct financial institution) would not commit to a firm selling price, we determined that the property would require approximately $10,000 in repairs.

We decided to buy the property—without knowing the price. But first, we needed to raise the money.

Four consecutive Sundays, I requested an additional $20 from each church member for the special need. Many of our people struggled to make ends meet and found it difficult to give to the church at all—but they did. This one-time offering collected $72,000.

When the FSLIC issued their $62,000 selling price for the property, we were right on target—$10,000 for repairs, and $62,000 for the building! As usual, God was far ahead of us.

There Is Such a Thing as a Free Lunch

Now that we had a building and a dream, we needed money to operate the outreach center and to feed 50 to 60 people daily. A few days after we acquired the building, a man who owns a sandwich vending business called on our church administrator, mentioning that he replenished his machines often to ensure sandwich freshness. If we could use them, he said, he would provide us with sandwiches enough for 50 to 60 people per day—the exact number we had estimated! I had been a pastor for 35 years, and this was the only time anyone ever offered to give food to our church.

It wasn't long before a member of the Green Acres congregation, the owner of a potato chip business, provided all the chips we needed. A local bakery contributed bread. Imagine all of this without a single request on our part!

The outreach center has been operating for almost three years. During its first year, 12,000 people were fed, 15,000 were clothed, and free medical and dental services helped 1,500 people. By the end of 1991, the church will have fed twice that number—some 24,000 people—clothed 28,000 people, and treated 2,400 people.

The same building houses The Good Samaritan Baptist Church, an African-American congregation. When the church was orga-

nized, Reggie Thomas, a student at Southwestern Baptist Theological Seminary, was called as pastor. Starting from ground zero,
Reggie baptized 57 converts the first year and built an attendance
of 172 in a facility that seats only 171. If Good Samaritan continues
its rapid growth, a family life center will soon be needed to serve the
church and surrounding community.

A New Day for an Old Church

The Sylvania Baptist Church was founded more than 40 years
ago. Once a thriving congregation with over 200 attending Sunday
School, through the years, attendance had declined to 20 people per
Sunday. Most of the remaining members were elderly, living on low
incomes, with little hope of the leadership the church needed. The
church had no teachers, musicians, or other types of workers.
Without outside assistance, Sylvania would eventually close.

Green Acres provided Sylvania with much-needed planning
and management. Some members were asked to move their
memberships to Sylvania and to assume leadership positions.
Green Acres provided the church with teachers, a minister of music,
a pianist, singers, and called Matthew McKellar to be pastor.   At
publication of this book Matthew was completing his Ph.D. degree
at Southwestern Baptist Theological Seminary in Fort Worth. With
the infusion of new life from Green Acres and the able leadership of
Matthew McKeller, Sylvania grew and, within three years, averaged 182 people in Sunday school. Sylvania's sanctuary and
fellowship hall were remodeled, a new educational building was
completed, a full-time minister of music is on staff, and the growth
continues. Two years later when I reconstituted Sylvania into an
independent church they had 415 in Sunday school. This is truly
a new day for an old church!

Even though I am no longer with Green Acres, they are always
in my prayers. What will come next? Where will it lead? I do not
know. I know the church is not content to sit and sing "Just As I Am"
to one another. It received a commission to reach out in an ever-
widening circle until the gospel was carried to the ends of the earth.

And, of this I am confident: when and where the Lord guides, he will provide. That's why we must make a great commotion about the Great Commission.

Statistically, 60 percent of Southern Baptist Churches have less than 300 members. What can a 300-member or a 200-member church do that is comparable to Green Acres? Win the lost. Feed the hungry. Clothe the poor. Shelter the homeless. Heal the sick. It's all relative. Can your church feed one hungry family? Then why not do it? Just because you cannot do everything is no excuse for doing nothing. Financially, the genius of cooperative giving is involvement of the smallest church in the biggest mission task the world has ever known.

8

Pray for the Lost:
The Right Way

Virtually anyone will tell you that prayer is essential to building an evangelistic church. Great and growing churches pray cooperatively and individually, in their Sunday services, mid-week prayer meetings, or all-night vigils. They have prayer retreats and prayer chains. They pray for the sick, for one another, for their national leaders.

However, as I have studied the New Testament, I realize praying for the lost is not the primary thrust of the New Testament with regard to evangelism. The Scriptures do not record that Jesus Christ ever prayed explicitly and directly for the salvation of a lost soul. Nor did he ever command us to do so. Instead, he taught us to pray for those who persecute us (Matthew 5:44), which might indirectly be perceived as praying for the lost. Praying over the city of Jerusalem, Jesus lamented, "Oh, Jerusalem, Jerusalem...how often would I have gathered thy children together, even as a hen gathereth her chickens under her wings, and ye would not!" (Matthew 23:37). This seems more of a lament for a city that has forfeited opportunity rather than a prayer for its salvation.

Neither Paul nor any of the other apostles urge us to pray for the lost. Paul did teach that we pray "for kings and all that are in authority" (1 Timothy 2:1-2), that government authorities would not inhibit the free working ot the church. God "will have all men to be saved, and to come unto the knowledge of the truth" (1 Timothy 2:4). Prayer for the unsaved is only implied, not specifi-

73

cally taught.

The most explicit prayer for the unsaved in the New Testament is Paul's cry, "Brethren, my heart's desire and prayer to God for Israel is, that they might be saved" (Romans 10:1). Yet even this is a prayer for the salvation of the entire nation rather than salvation for individual Jews.

This is amazing, especially in light of the fact that our ministers and churches seem to encourage us to pray for the lost. Yet, if we are not commanded to pray for the lost, what does the New Testament teach in regard to prayer and evangelism?

When Jesus saw the vast spiritual need and evangelistic potential of the times, he said to his disciples: "The harvest truly is plenteous, but the labourers are few; pray ye therefore the Lord of the harvest, that he will send forth labourers into his harvest" (Matthew 9:37-38).

Thus, the primary thrust of the New Testament was established. Jesus emphasized the harvesters rather than the harvest, laborers rather than the lost, saints rather than sinners. At the time Jesus spoke these words, there were 7,200 priests who ministered at the temple and 9,600 Levites. But while they practiced the rituals of temple worship, the world perished for want of personal reconciliation with God. Jesus then urged us to pray for more workers.

The word that Jesus chose, translated from the Greek as "send forth," emphatically means to "thrust forth." It is the same word chosen to describe Jesus' "casting out" of demons and Jesus' "driving out" of moneychangers who had turned the temple of God into a place of commerce. Jesus taught us to pray for people to feel compelled—or sent forth—to work in the over-ripe harvest fields.

In much the same way, God thrusts people—pastors and laypersons alike—into the ministry. And there is a close correlation between our praying and his sending. As a teenager, I felt a strong urge to preach. When I consented to the Lord, I thought this decision was between God and me alone. But when I told others of my decision, my mother revealed that, for years, she had prayed that I would be a preacher. And the dear people at my church said, "We knew God would call you. We've been praying to that end."

Several years ago, our church became concerned that so few of our young people were committing their lives to Christian service. So we prayed that God would send young people out from our fellowship into the ministry. Our prayers were answered in a short time, for more young people surrendered their lives to Christian service than any time in our church's history.

Likewise, our missionaries in Belize prayed that God would call upon young Belizian nationals to become pastors and evangelists. As a result of their intense prayers and three days of preaching, 14 young men stepped forward, testifying that God had called them to preach.

In his writings, the Apostle Paul expressed much the same sentiment as Jesus. When Paul landed in jail, he requested prayer from believers in two local churches. He encouraged the church at Ephesus to pray "for all saints; And for me, that utterance may be given unto me, that I may open my mouth boldly, to make known the mystery of the gospel" (Ephesians 6:19). He also wrote to the church at Colosse: "Continue in prayer...praying also for us, that God would open unto us a door of utterance, to speak the mystery of Christ, for which I am also in bonds: That I may make it manifest, as I ought to speak" (Colossians 4:2-4).

These passages, similar in content, offer valuable insight into the nature of "harvester" praying and indicate that the emphasis of the New Testament centers on praying for the harvesters, laborers and saints, as opposed to the harvest, the lost and the sinners.

For instance, suppose you were tossed in jail, surrounded by guards and other prisoners, all in desperate need of Christ. You then decide to write your local church, requesting prayer. What would you ask? You would likely mention the names of those hardened prisoners serving time with you, and ask your fellow Christians to pray that God would soften their hearts and save them. Yet Paul, in such a situation, requested that believers pray on his behalf. He, too, felt that prayer should be devoted to the saint rather than the sinner: that is, prayer for his own effectiveness in witnessing for Christ.

It is, of course, not wrong to pray for the lost; in fact, it is right that we should pray for them, but we must not let praying for the lost be a substitute for witnessing to them. When we care about people, we cannot help but pray, "God save my son," or "Lord, save my neighbor," or "Father, save Bill." They need our prayers, but they also need our witness. We must give them both.

These passages, taken from Paul's letters, interpret Christ's command to pray for workers to be sent into the harvest. This, I believe, is the right way to pray for the lost. And, it is, I believe, an emphasis that needs to be recovered by our churches today. Let's take a closer look, then, at the passages, for this is the primary thrust of the New Testament relative to prayer and evangelism.

Pray For Open Doors

First, we should pray for opportunities to witness. Paul did not request prayer to deliver him from prison or to relieve a stressful situation. He asked that churches pray "that God would open up unto us a door of utterance, to speak the mystery of Christ" (Colossians 4:3). The open door metaphor is often used in scripture to represent an entrance or opportunity (Acts 14:27; 1 Corinthians 16:9; 2 Corinthians 2:12; Revelation 3:8). Here, Paul requests an opportunity to witness.

We must understand God's part and our part in evangelism. The Bible makes it clear that God is responsible for opening the door of opportunity. And we should not force an opportunity by battering, kicking, or beating on the door. Through our prayers, God knows to provide us with an open door. But once God does open the door, then it becomes our responsibility as Christians to pass through it and bear witness to the saving grace of God in Christ.

One might rationalize, however, "The best way to do that is by example. I will just live my witness and not speak it." A noble thought, but our faith is vastly different from our lives—even though, as Christians, we try to make our lives as consistent with our faith as possible. That is why the word of witness is so important—and why it is so important that all Christians know their faith as well as some theology, and can give witness to their belief in Jesus.

Also, the verbal witness is a bold discipline. When we directly confront someone with the gospel there is an inherent invitation for that person to observe the work of the gospel in our own lives. This invitation to watch becomes a strong reminder to speak and act in ways that reflect Christ.

So we must live good lives and simultaneously search for opportunities to witness. If we look and pray, opportunities will come, for everyone has a problem or knows of one. One word of caution, however: seize these opportunities. They will not last forever. Open doors do close.

Pray For Courage

Second, we should pray for the courage to witness. Paul twice requested prayer to speak the mystery of the gospel "boldly" (Ephesians 6:19-20).

The Greek word for boldness literally means outspokenness, frankness, bluntness. We recognize, however, that Christians should never be blunt or brash in their witnessing, but kind, respectful and considerate. In the sense of Christian evangelism, boldness means fearlessness or unashamed liberty. Paul, then, prays for the ability to witness fearlessly, the ability to present the gospel unaffected by hesitancy or anxiety.

Boldness has always characterized God's people. The bold witness of Peter and John, for instance, convinced Jewish leaders in Jerusalem that the two men had been with Jesus. After the crippled man at the temple had been miraculously healed, the leaders threatened the disciples and demanded that they not speak in the name of Jesus. Later that evening during prayer, the disciples called upon the Lord: "And now, Lord, behold their threatenings: and grant unto thy servants, that with all boldness they may speak thy word" (Acts 4:29). Instead of deliverance or vengeance, Peter and John prayed for boldness in order that they might speak for Christ, even in the face of certain persecution.

The single greatest obstacle to our evangelism is fear. If the apostles Paul, Peter and John requested prayer for boldness, fear must have been an obstacle for them. We, too, must overcome fear as an obstacle and pray for the boldness to speak freely and unashamedly about Jesus Christ.

Norman Nix, an Australian Baptist leader, said of his country-men, "The only people who aren't ashamed to use the name of Jesus in Australia are unbelievers." This is equally true of Americans. Nonbelievers shamelessly use his name in vain, while we Christians are far too often silenced by fear.

Why is there hesitation to speak freely and candidly about Jesus Christ? Whatever the reason may be, it is there. It is there for me. It must also have been there for Paul, and that's why he requested prayer for "boldness."

Prayer calms our fears and transforms us into bold witnesses. Therefore, we should pray for the Lord to open doors of opportunity so that we might witness—as well as the courage to speak freely about our Lord. Otherwise, we will miss countless golden opportunities.

Henry Ford once purchased a sizeable insurance policy on his life. Because of Ford's prominence and the amount of the policy, the newspapers took notice. After reading of the purchase, one of Ford's friends, an insurance salesman, confronted Ford and asked why the policy had not been purchased from him. Ford's simple reply was, "You never asked me."

Several years ago, a young lady was elected to serve as a member of our youth staff during "Youth Week." As was the custom in our church, the full-time staff person she represented accompanied her on a visitation assignment. To become better acquainted during their visit, he asked her, "When did you join our church?"

She responded, "I haven't joined yet."

Surprised by her answer, he asked, "Why not?"

"Nobody ever asked me," she replied. He did and she did.

There are many people like Henry Ford and our Youth Week staff member. They are waiting to be asked. We must not let them down. We need to pray that the Lord will not only open doors of opportunity for us to witness, but also for the courage to open our mouths and witness.

Keep It Simple

Third, we should pray for clarity in witnessing. Paul begged his readers to pray " ... that utterance may be given unto me..." (Ephesians 6:19). Used here, "utterance" is the Greek word logos, meaning word, something to say, a topic, a message. The Apostle Paul wanted not only an opportunity and the boldness to witness, he also wanted a clear message to "be given" to him by God: "That I may make it manifest, as I ought to speak" (Colossians 4:4).

In these passages, Paul refers to "the mystery of the gospel" (Ephesians 6:19) and "the mystery of Christ" (Colossians 4:3). A "mystery" in the biblical sense is not only difficult, but impossible to understand except through revelation. Paul's request for prayer is that he be granted the opportunity and courage to preach with sufficient simplicity and clarity to reach people for the Savior. In both instances, Paul implies that the clarity he seeks is beyond human capability and only possible through the working of the Holy Spirit.

In essence, Paul wanted God to give him a message and the ability to share it with others in such a way that it would be understood and received. Paul perceived that such effective witnessing must be initiated and substantiated by God, and that the Holy Spirit must wield the sword if conviction and conversion are to occur. Obviously, Paul felt prayer necessary to accomplish this.

A budding young author once brought his novel to H. G. Wells for evaluation. When Wells returned the young man's manuscript, he had penciled these words on the corner: "Boy, you have a style, but you don't have a story." We have a story, but we must pray for a style to share it effectively.

Frank Pollard relates that when he was a pastor in West Texas, a member of his congregation asked him to visit her husband. She confessed that her husband drank heavily and was physically abusive. Frank reluctantly sought out their little, unpainted farm house in the country. He knocked on the wobbly front door, and the man answered, outfitted in blue jeans, white T-shirt, with beer in hand. They sat at the kitchen table where Frank began to share the "Roman road" to salvation with him. At first, the man showed no interest in spiritual matters. But, as Frank continued to witness and read the Scripture, the man's demeanor changed. He eventually asked Frank, "Isn't there something in there about a book and a man's name being written in it?"

Frank replied, "Yes, there is." He quickly turned to the Book of Revelation and read, "And whosever was not found written in the book of life was cast into the lake of fire" (Revelation 20:15).

The man rose from his chair, leaned across the table, looked Frank in the eye, and said, "Preacher, I want my name in that book."

When we witness in the power of the Holy Spirit, something akin to this often happens: conviction and conversion occur. That's why we must pray for "utterance" and the ability to speak his word plainly.

Real evangelism, then, begins not by talking to people about God, but by talking to God about people, crying to God about sending workers to the harvest. If you know people who are lost in sin, pray that God give you courage to witness to them. If a loved one is lost, pray that God will usher a Christian into his life and for that Christian to witness effectively to your loved one.

This is "harvest" praying at its fullest—absolutely essential to building a great evangelistic church. Go forward!

9

Be Fit for the Master's Use

An old bishop in India was approached by a missionary who asked, "Bishop, I have sought a deeper experience with God all these years, and I don't have it. I have read books about what to do, and I have kept all the rules, but I am nowhere yet. Does God have favorites?"

The old bishop replied, "No, my dear, God does not have favorites. But he does have intimates."

God is no respecter of persons, but he is a respecter of character and has an affinity for the pure in heart. A number of the scriptures reflect this. In Psalm 24, David wrote, "Who shall ascend into the hill of the Lord? or who shall stand in his holy place? He that hath clean hands, and a pure heart..." (Psalm 24:3-4). And Jesus taught that "Blessed are the pure in heart: for they shall see God" (Matthew 5:8). Perhaps the most candid passage concerning the importance of a pure heart is found in the second Epistle of Timothy.

"But in a great house there are not only vessels of gold and of silver, but also of wood and of earth; and some to honour, and some to dishonour. If a man therefore purge himself from these, he shall be a vessel unto honour, sanctified, and meet for the master's use, and prepared unto every good work" (2 Timothy 2:20-21).

Wedged between appeals to pure living, this is a simple illustration of a profound, eternal truth. It is this: purity (integrity, character) is prerequisite for achieving usefulness in God's service. Five truths found in these verses will help us to understand this better.

First, the church is often compared to a large house or mansion.

Peter speaks of the church as a "spiritual house" (1 Peter 2:5), and Paul wrote to Timothy telling him how to behave in "the house of God" (1 Timothy 3:15).

Second, believers are compared to dishes or eating utensils within the house, a common analogy in the Scriptures. The Lord called the Apostle Paul "a chosen vessel" (Acts 9:15). Peter refers to the wife as the "weaker vessel" (1 Peter 3:7). And Paul wrote in reference to the gospel, "But we have this treasure in earthen vessels..." (2 Corinthians 4:7). The riches of God's grace are entrusted to ordinary people like you and me—all chosen vessels, weak vessels, earthen vessels, say the scriptures.

Third, there is a rich variety of vessels present in God's house: some gold, some silver, still others wood or clay. A poor man's house will have one kind of dish, while a mansion or king's palace would have many different types. My family had a single set of dishes to use for all occasions. Many affluent homes today have pottery and plastic, paper plates and fine china—whatever the occasion requires.

All these different vessels—gold, silver, wood and clay— represent the many people of God's house.

Fourth, the highest honor and the greatest joy of Christian life is to be used by God in his service. Paul notes that some vessels are "to honour" and some "to dishonour," meaning that some are reserved for special occasions, others are used every day. Some are for the master's use, others are used by servants. Only the best vessels would be used by the king; and to be used by the king would be the greatest honor a vessel could have. To be used by God in his service is the greatest joy and highest honor a Christian worker can know.

Finally, cleanliness is prerequisite for usefulness to God and service in his kingdom. It is not important that we be silver-tongued orators or golden-throated singers. What really matters most in God's service? That our lives be clean. As Paul wrote to Timothy, "If a man therefore purge himself ... he shall be a vessel unto honour ... meet for the master's use ... " (2 Timothy 2:21).

When you eat, what is important about the dishes set before you? It matters little that the dishes are china, pottery, plastic or paper. The size, shape, color or cost is of no real importance either. But what is important is their cleanliness. Who wants to eat from a dirty plate with dirty utensils? You wouldn't, nor would God. The challenge issued by this text, then, is that we purge ourselves of impurity so that we may be fit for the Lord's use.

The word "purge," meaning to cleanse, is used 29 times in the Bible. In 27 of those references, "purge" describes an act of God; in only two instances, "purge" describes what we must do.

We must purge ourselves, as Paul writes to Timothy (2 Timothy 2:21). And also according to Paul, the church must purify itself: "Purge out therefore the old leaven" (1 Corinthians 5:7).

An anonymous critic once commented, "The church today is like Noah's ark: if it weren't for the storm on the outside, you couldn't stand the stench on the inside." The Spirit of God cannot abide in the midst of such uncleanliness, and that is why the church is commanded to purge itself.

No word could prove more appropriate today, for our profession has suffered through many scandals. The passage instructs us as individuals and—especially as ministers—to cleanse ourselves of sin so that we may offer the greatest usefulness to God. To be successful in the ministry, we must rid our lives of immoral acts, deceit, and sinful pride.

Someone Has to Be Good

First of all, we must purge our lives of immorality. Several years ago, a man and his wife joined the church where I was pastor. Before making the change, the man explained the reason. As coach of his church's softball team, the man had returned the sports equipment to the church one hot summer afternoon. The pastor was mowing the parsonage lawn, next door to the church. When the pastor spotted him wiping the sweat from his brow, he shouted, "John, when you get through come on over, and we'll have a cold beer."

John said, "Right then, I decided we had to get out of that church." Then he added, "Preacher, someone in this world has to be good."

In light of John's remarks, I thought of a line from Chaucer's Canterbury Tales: "If gold rusts, what will iron do?" ("Prologue," line 500). If God's ministers are not good, what influence could we possibly have on unbelievers or even our own people?

Sir Galahad was perhaps the noblest knight of King Arthur's legendary Round Table, having the most important role in the search for the Holy Grail, the cup from which Christ supposedly drank at the Last Supper. Sir Galahad was depicted by Tennyson as the ideal young man, set apart from others by his strength and purity.

> *My good blade curves the casque of men*
> *My tough lance thrusteth sure,*
> *My strength is the strength of ten*
> *Because my heart is pure.*

Likewise, our power with God and our usefulness to him are linked directly to the purity of our lives. If we are to be useful at all to God as ministers, we must give up our lax ways and return to holy living.

Elsewhere, to become a pastor means living up to scrutiny of both God and man. In the Soviet Union, for instance, pastoral candidates are questioned thoroughly, and their lives as well as theological views are studied by local church leaders and the congregation prior to ordination.

"When we consider a candidate," explains Jacob Dukahonchenka, superintendent of Evangelical Christian Baptists in the Ukraine, "we observe not only preaching ability, but we search his life and his spiritual side. Living the gospel is imperative."

Dukahonchenka recalls a story about Radstock, a founder of the evangelical movement in nineteenth century Russia. When Radstock was preaching about Christ one day, a cabman standing outside the hall heard the sermon. The cabman asked a man leaving the service, "Do you know the preacher?"

"Yes," the man replied.

"Does the preacher live as beautifully as he preaches?" the cabman queried.

"No," responded the man, "he could not preach so beautifully as he lives."

Said Dukahonchenka, "We are not ignorant of the meaning of the sermon, but we value very much the life of the preacher." If we are to achieve usefulness to God and build bigger, better churches, we must live more beautifully than we preach. The prayer of the psalmist should also be ours: "Let the words of my mouth, and the meditation of my heart, be acceptable in thy sight, O Lord, my strength, and my redeemer" (Psalm 19:14).

The Lord Comes First

Second, we need to purge our lives of deceit. General Dean, of Korean War fame, wrote a letter to his wife shortly before he died. In his letter, he included a message to his young son in case he (Dean) did not return from the war: "Tell Mark, integrity is the word, integrity is the word."

Integrity was not only the word for little Mark, it is also the word for ministers. Exaggeration, misrepresentation and deceit are common among us today.

Sometimes our dishonesty stems from excessive ambition and competitiveness. I heard of two preachers who, while hiking, looked behind them only to see a big black bear "bearing down" on them. One of the preachers sat down, took off his hiking boots, and slipped on his jogging shoes. The other preacher looked at him and said, "I don't know why you're doing that. You can't outrun that bear whether you have on your hiking boots or your jogging shoes."

He continued to tie his shoes as he retorted, "I don't have to outrun that bear. I just have to outrun you."

In our desire to outrun one another—to sign up the largest number of new members or log the greatest attendance in Sunday School or to baptize more people than the next church—some pastors stretch the truth, pad their records, even falsify reports. They "need" to exceed their fellow pastors, being the biggest and the best, and willing to pay the price of dishonesty.

We should not attempt to race with one another, for we are on a pilgrimage. We should not try to best someone else, for we are trying to reach as many people with the gospel as possible. We should not be competitors, for we are fellow servants of Christ. We need the spirit of the missionary who prayed, "Lord, I care not who is second, so long as Thou art first."

We must have integrity in our reporting. During World War II in the Battle of Britain, Sir Winston Churchill gathered the Royal Air Force pilots to impress on them the importance of accuracy. His words are just as meaningful to us as ministers today, as we wage the battle for God's kingdom.

"In your eagerness to win the war, you are in danger of losing it for us because you are exaggerating the truth. We have been depending on the accuracy of your statements after your flights at the briefing sessions. But we have discovered that oftentimes not so many planes were shot down, and not so many war targets were bombed as you reported. Please gentlemen, be as factual and as accurate in your figures as possible" (Manchester, p. 327).

The Humble Don't Stumble

Third, we need to purge our lives of sinful pride. Of the two kinds of pride, one makes a person want to look his best, be his best, and do his best. The other, sinful pride, causes us to shamelessly strut before God and view others with disdain. Jesus once related a parable of the Publicans and the Pharisees that illustrates how sinful pride behaves: "And he spake this parable unto certain which trusted in themselves that they were righteous, and despised others" (Luke 18:9).

In our professional lives, pride can cause us to be pompous and conceited, telling the world of grand achievements and the great success of our churches. Although we may think that such boasting makes us look good, it actually reflects our own insecurities.

Oscar-winning actor, Gregory Peck, stood in line at a restaurant, waiting for the acknowledgement of an arrogant maitre d'. Someone said to Peck, "Why don't you tell him who you are?"

Peck responded, "When you have to tell them, you aren't."

We would do well to remember Willie Lohman from Arthur Millers' "Death of a Salesman." Willie had been convinced that

Bernard, his neighbor's son, would never amount to anything. Bernard grew up, and while packing his bags for a trip, chats with Willie. After Bernard has departed, Willie discovers that the young man is travelling to Washington to plead a case before the Supreme Court. Willie is surprised. "What do you know?" he exclaims. "Bernard didn't even say anything about it."

Says Bernard's father, "He didn't have to; he is doing it."

A church that moves from success to success, a preacher that moves from victory to victory, or a denomination that moves from height to height need not advertise achievements.

In our personal lives, pride can make us over confident and vulnerable. In the wake of a recent sex scandal involving a prominent pastor, pastoral counselor Peter Stienke observed: "Clergy who become involved in affairs most often are people who exude self-confidence and are self-assured, charming and very success-ful."

Tracing the behavioral pattern of many ministers who become involved in sexual affairs, Stienke pointed out that, in some ways, they are persons with strong narcissistic traits. (In Greek mythology, Narcissus was a handsome youth who fell in love with his own reflection in a pool of water; he remained there, transfixed by his own image, until he died.)

Narcissistic people, Stienke says, are those "whose inner life isn't well developed, and they live their lives in the outer world." But because they are charming and successful, he says, they "project an image and people gravitate to them."

People often become attracted to this type of pastor, Stienke states, when they are insecure due to a floundering marriage, a lack of fulfillment at work, or some other self-image problem. It is easy for a narcissistic personality to "use people, manipulate them, use their charm—it's gotten them this far," Stienke points out. Perhaps there is a problem in the minister's own marriage, and the relation-ship with a different person can become "playful and make them feel whole, complete...It's the strong, dealing with the weak."

Often, maybe because of a vacuum in his own marriage, the minister turns to other sources of recognition and becomes "over-worked and overcommitted" and thereby "sets himself up for an affair," Stienke says.

Stienke concludes that, interestingly enough, these ministers often believe they are in control of their emotions and are unaware of their dependency.

Although the headline may be fresh, it's really the same old story; they fall because they view themselves above temptation. The Scriptures are right: "Wherefore let him that thinketh he standeth take heed lest he fall" (1 Corinthians 10:12).

Ila Ann Gary, the widow of a long-time Baptist preacher, advised me more than once to "Stay humble, so you don't stumble." The scriptures offer the same warning: "Pride goeth before destruction, and an haughty spirit before a fall" (Proverbs 16:18).

Here is the solemn fact: if we do not cleanse ourselves, we invite the punitive cleansing of God. The second book of Kings bears this out, for when God begins cleansing, he does a thorough job: "...and I will wipe Jerusalem as a man wipeth a dish, wiping it, and turning it upside down" (2 Kings 21:13).

We don't want him to chasten and purge us. He invites us to first, cleanse ourselves, so that we may prove useful within his kingdom.

But how do we purge ourselves? First, by committing ourselves to Christ. In Shakespeare's play, Macbeth entreats the court physician to treat his wife, Lady Macbeth, who was suffering from guilt and "anguish of her soul." The physician explains that Lady Macbeth's disease is beyond his ability, and "Therein the patient must minister to himself" (Macbeth V iii).

According to the Book of Hebrews, Jesus "by himself purged our sins" (Hebrews 1:3), preparing us for cleansing and forgiveness.

Second, we need continued cleansing through confession. The Scriptures say that "If we confess our sins, he is faithful and just to forgive us our sins and to cleanse us from all unrighteousness" (1 John 1:9).

We know what our sins are, for God convicts us of them both in Scripture and in conscience. If we want our lives to be cleansed, we must first come clean with God. It is prerequisite to our usefulness and essential to being a successful pastor in a stressful world.

The late James Irwin, one of America's first astronauts, then an evangelist, wrote in his book, "*More Than Earthlings*," about the first Russian cosmonaut, who returned from outer space, then travelled the world declaring that he looked, but never saw God out in space. A young Swedish girl, remembering the words of Jesus—"Blessed are the pure in heart, for they shall see God"— wrote him a letter that said: "Dear Sir, I understand when you were out in space you looked around and you said you never saw God. Sir, I just want to ask you one question, 'Is your heart pure?'" (Irwin, p. 83). Go Forward!

10

Prioritize Your Preaching

Preaching provides the pastor with not only his greatest opportunity, but also his greatest challenge. Preaching offers opportunity because it is the primary way he feeds and leads his congregation. Through his words, he communicates love, warmth, concern and truth.

Preaching becomes a challenge because, seated before him, are the diverse "children" who must be fed on the "milk of the word": inquiring teenagers, skeptical college students, academicians, widows and widowers, harried homemakers, the aged and dying, the burdened, defeated, depressed, disappointed, indifferent, self-righteous and the complacent—and the list goes on. All sit before the preacher, waiting to hear some word from the Lord that applies to their own situation. And, in my denomination, the typical pastor is expected to have that word at least 150 times per year! Perhaps such a challenge prompted Ruskin to say, "The preacher has on Sunday morning thirty minutes to raise the dead."

In many ways, preaching is a barometer of the life of the church. When preaching is dynamic, the church is strong; when preaching is lackluster, the church is weak and anemic. With preaching, the church grows or it declines.

Several years ago, at a conference on expository preaching held in California, Ray Steadman said that more than 75 percent of the churches in America are no longer growing or are actually experiencing a decline in membership. The primary reason cited is the "boring and irrelevant worship services."

Speaking at the same conference, sociologist Oz Guiness said, "I have never seen a western society where the church pews are so full and the sermons are so empty."

Because preaching is so important in the life of the church, the pastor who wants to build a great evangelistic church must devote attention to the planning, preparation, presentation and preservation of his sermons.

Planning to Preach

Basically an expository preacher, I like to preach through books of the Bible, building my sermons on two or more verses of Scripture and drawing the points directly from the text. This kind of preaching gives me a sense of accomplishment as I progress through a book of the Bible; it forces me to deal wth subjects I would otherwise pass over; and it helps me avoid a frantic search for the right subject to address the next Sunday. I simply preach what comes next in the book. After all, that's the way the Lord gave it to us, and it is all inspired.

Not a slave to expository preaching, I deviate from it readily when necessary. Thus, in a year's time, my preaching covers the gamut of styles: topical, textual, biographical and expository.

For the other types of sermons, I continually collect ideas, titles, texts and outlines for future use from a number of activities: my own devotional time, general reading, listening to or talking with other preachers, and personal experience. These are placed in a folder marked "Sermon Ideas," becoming the seeds for future sermons.

Preparing to Preach

Monday morning, first thing, I would choose a title and text for my next sermon. Next follows critical examination of the text to determine its full and correct meaning. Several biblical commentaries as well as "*The New Strong's Exhaustive Concordance*" help me derive meaning from the passages and offers insight into the Greek and Hebrew languages.

Once the exegesis is completed, a thesis and working outline have generally emerged. From my viewpoint, both are essential to effective preaching.

The thesis consists of a one-sentence statement which summarizes what I wish to say to my listeners. J. H. Jowett emphasized the importance of a thesis when he said that no man was really prepared to preach until he could summarize his message in one simple, well-formed sentence. I agree, for I can make clear to my listeners only what is crystal clear to me.

When Norman Vincent Peale began preaching, his father required that he send him, each Saturday night, a 10-word telegram which summarized his sermon for the next day. Every preacher could derive benefit from such a discipline.

Just as important as the thesis is the outline. Like a nail, the thesis is the truth I want to drive home to my listeners. My outline points are like the blows of a hammer, driving the thesis ever deeper into the minds and hearts of my listeners. My points are definitive, my language spare, so that they may be remembered easily. And I repeat points often for emphasis in my sermon.

A good approach to public speaking is like that of Winston Churchill. Take one idea and give it a whack! Talk awhile, then give your idea another whack! Talk a little more, then give it yet another whack! When it's time for the finale, give it a terrific whack! (Pollard, p. 72).

Most of my sermons involve three points, which naturally divide as the result of time and logic. I try not to force points, but instead let them flow directly from the text or the thesis.

Once my outline is in place, I search for illustrations. Each point of the sermon would contain three elements: exegesis, illustration, and application. Exegesis seeks to reveal God's exact message. Application makes divine truth practical for the listener. Illustration, like windows, lets in the light and fresh air, making the sermon understandable and interesting.

A good illustration ranges from a full-length story, like the parable of the prodigal son, to a quotation or one-line zinger. What could be more vivid that Vance Havner's description of the instability of some Christians: "They go up like a rocket and down like a rock; they begin with a fever and end up with a chill." Or Mark

Twain on the importance of using the right word: "The difference between the right word and the almost right word is the difference between lightning and a lightning bug." Save illustration, no single element has the power to transform a poor sermon into a good one or a good sermon into a better one.

Finding illustrations is easy, once you develop an eye for them. And they're everywhere! It does require discipline, but if you train yourself to see and hear them, then work to preserve them, you'll never want for a supply of good material.

Always carrying pen and paper makes recording stories, quotations, inspirational flashes or humor a simple matter. The best advice on illustrations is to write them down as they occur—don't trust your memory.

I file materials according to alphabet and topic. File folders marked "A" through "Z" hold materials on more general subjects; specific topics command their own folders designated alcohol, atheism, assurance, age, apologetics, etc. Once I determine my sermon subject, I leaf through the appropriate file folder and often discover far more material than I can use.

The conclusion—tying up the threads of the sermon—usually emerges naturally as the sermon develops. For me, the conclusion should reach a spiritual climax with an evangelistic appeal and invitation to Christ, thus bringing all main points into sharp focus.

The final decision I make is what really comes first in the sermon. A current event, story, quotation or personal experience will capture listeners' attention and hold their interest as I introduce my message. No matter how full of truth a sermon may be, if it is not compelling or interesting enough to seize the listeners' attention, it will make no impact or do little good.

Presenting the Sermon

Early in my ministry, I scripted each sermon in full. Although a valuable discipline, scripting became more and more difficult as my pastoral responsibilities increased. Now I outline my sermons fully—rather than write them—and preach from my notes.

My notes prove most effective written on a folded 8 1/2" x 11" sheet of paper. Placed over the pages of my Bible adjacent to the text of the sermon, with notes on both sides of the pages, I can hold my Bible, glancing at my notes easily and inconspicuously as I preach.

By the time I am ready to preach, I am well acquainted with my outline and illustrations, so that I am not tied to my notes, and I can speak freely while maintaining eye contact with my listeners. I believe that people want to hear a preacher who will stand up, look them directly in the eye, and speak as though he believes in what he says. As Will Rogers once said, "I don't like to hear a preacher read his sermon. I always think, if he can't remember it, how does he expect me to?"

While preaching, I offer introduction and text, then enumerate points simply and clearly. As I develop the sermon and move from point to point, I repeat each previous point for emphasis, clarity and continuity. I try to follow the dictum I learned somewhere: Keep it simple, say it often, make it burn.

12 Tips on Preaching

Here are some practical suggestions for communicating your message, learned over 35 years of preaching the gospel.

1. *Keep it simple.* The great Billy Sunday expressed his views on preaching to a group of young ministers: "Don't preach always to the intellectual giraffes in the congregation. Leave some fodder on the bottom shelf for the calves."

"Aim the gospel at simplicity," says Billy Graham. "You don't have to be profound. You can say profound things in simple ways. Read Moody's sermons. He had one story after another: a lot of deathbed stories, simple language. But Britain and America listened, and they will listen today if it's preached with authority and simplicity" (Graham, p. 23).

2. *Keep it short.* On the pulpit at the Pine Springs Baptist Church, outside Tyler, Texas, are printed these words: "Lord, fill my mouth with wonderful stuff, then nudge me when I've said enough." Clergy suffer many jokes over their verbosity. But when sermons "never stop," it is no laughing matter. General George C. Patton was right: "To be talked to death is a terrible way to die." In this swiftly

changing society, the speaker who can state the facts succinctly, or quickly inspire listeners to action, possesses an invaluable skill.

3. *Address people's needs.* Steinbeck's "*The Grapes of Wrath*" portrays a preacher, Casey, who, in his travels about the countryside, discovers countless empty houses. Families are moving west. Casey decides he must also leave "to go where folks is going." Pastoral preaching is specific in that it attempts to deal with where people are in their lives. Today, people are not interested in studying early worship in the catacombs; they seek survival in the subways and life among the skyscrapers. As one brother said, "We are not interested in pie in the sky by and by, we want chicken in the kitchen tonight. I want ham where I am today!"

4. *Say it with passion.* Years ago, someone asked Charles Haddon Spurgeon, "How can I communicate like you do?"

"It's very simple," he answered. "Pour some kerosene over you, light a match, and people will come to watch you burn."

Woodrow Wilson said it this way: "Where there is fire, thither will men carry their lamps to be lighted."

5. *Preach to the heart.* We aren't all intellectuals, but we do have hearts. "Aim at people's head," R. G. Lee once said, "and you might miss. Aim at their heart and you'll hit them every time."

A chaplain had been conducting services for sailors. At the close, one of the men said to him, "That was a great sermon, preacher."

"Tell me," said the chaplain, "just why you think it was a great sermon."

After a moment's thought, the sailor replied, "It was a great sermon because you took something from you heart and put it in mine." That's the heart of bona fide preaching, for eloquence always touches emotions.

6. *Let your humanity show.* Including a "confessional element" in every sermon has proven to be a wise pastoral strategy, since many church members feel pastors are less than human and don't understand their problems. Through preaching, we have the opportunity to build relationships through strategic and tasteful self-disclosure.

7. *Use humor.* A long-recognized way of building speaker-

audience rapport, humor breaks down barriers, builds trust, and creates an atmosphere of response. Herb Gardner identified the evil of manipulation when he observed, "Once you get people laughing, they're listening and you can tell them almost anything."

Most notable preachers use humor effectively. The renowned preacher of London, Charles Haddon Spurgeon, was one of them. Spurgeon loved life; his favorite sound was laughter. In the pulpit, he often leaned back, roaring loudly over something he found amusing. When fellow clergymen, incensed by Spurgeon's humorous bent, railed against him, he responded with a chuckle: "If only you knew how much I hold back, you would commend me. This preacher thinks it less a crime to cause a momentary laughter than a half-hour of profound slumber."

How great was Spurgeon's humor? Addressing a preaching class on the importance of coordinating facial expression and speech, he advised, "When you speak of heaven, let your face light up, let it be irradiated with a heavenly gleam, let your eyes shine with reflective glory. But when you speak of hell—well, your ordinary face will do."

Of course, balance between the serious and the humorous is important. As Bishop Gerald Kennedy once said, "There is no harm in laughter. The preacher with a good sense of humor ought to use it in the pulpit, but always with restraint."

8. *Put your whole self into the sermon.* A young preacher was having no success in his church, so he asked the Bishop what was wrong. The Bishop asked him, "Are you tired when you get through preaching?"

The young man replied, "No, I feel fine and relaxed."

The Bishop said, "Young man, when you preach, somebody gets tired—either you do or the people do."

The weariness that follows heartfelt preaching does not result from pulpit gymnastics or contrived enthusiasm. A weariness of the soul, it results from carrying eternal truth in earthen vessels.

An elderly black preacher once gave a summation of great preaching technique. Asked how he always managed to preach such powerful sermons, he said, "It's easy. I just studies myself full, I thinks myself clear. I prays myself hot. And then I just lets go!"

9. *Leave them with hope.* Some time ago, I read a statement that greatly influenced my sermons: "When you preach, never leave Christ on the cross or the prodigal son in the far-country. Because Jesus returned from the grave, the prodigal son can come home again." Christ came back; so can we. Because Christ's tomb and cross are empty, our future can be filled with love, hope and happiness. Give people hope.

10. *Be evangelistic.* When the church service ended, a man spoke with the preacher concerning the sermon, concluding that "There was one thing lacking." The preacher asked what that was, and the man said:

"I am a Jew. I have recently been born again. Up until that time I had been to the synagogue. There was really nothing in your sermon that I could not have heard in the synagogue. Nothing that a Jewish rabbi might not have preached." Years later, the preacher confessed, "That was the greatest lesson in homiletics I was ever taught."

We must proclaim the good news to people and tell them how to be saved. The world does not need a better philosophy, a new morality, or reformation. The world needs a savior, a new life, and regeneration in Christ. Jesus said, "...if I be lifted up from the earth, will draw all men unto me." In the cross of Christ, there is an attraction that will bring devotion to the church and sinners to repentance and faith. If we preach the Christ of the cross, then, we shall see the world kneel at his feet.

11. *Preach for a verdict.* A young minister read one of his sermons to the Bishop, who listened in stony silence. The fearful clergyman then asked, "Will that do?"

The Bishop retorted sharply, "Do what? Preaching won't do unless it tells people what to do."

A good sermon is like a lawyer's brief: it is intended to gain a verdict. As one preacher said, "It is not my purpose to amuse you, abuse you, or confuse you but to infuse you." Like the end of your pencil—your sermon should have a point.

12. *Preach with urgency.* "I preach as never sure to preach again, as a dying man to dying men." (Baxter, p. 112)

Preserving a sermon.

Recording a sermon, then typing it in manuscript form allows me to save those moments of inspiration for future use. Once I have preached a sermon, I often discover illustrations, quotes, and insights that would serve to enrich and greatly improve it; these, I place in the appropriate file with the original manuscript. This allows a good sermon to grow, mature, and become much improved the next time it is preached.

Although some think you should never preach the same sermon more than once, my feeling is that if it is worth preaching once, it is worth preaching again. Just make sure it was worth preaching the first time.

"You know," boasted one man, "I've never preached the same sermon twice."

Someone overheard him and replied, "Well, I heard one of them once, and I don't blame him."

R. G. Lee preached his famous sermon "Payday Some Day" hundreds of times; it never seemed to grow old, even though it took more than an hour to deliver.

Powers of the Sermon

I can say of myself what Samuel Chadwick admitted: I would rather pay to preach than to be paid not to preach.

"Preaching has its price in agony of sweat and tears," said Chadwick. "No calling has such heartbreak, but preaching is a calling an archangel might covet. Thank God that by his grace he called me into the ministry of preaching" (Chadwick, p. 12).

Give attention to preaching. It's one of the keys to building a great evangelistic church. Go forward!

Appendix I

Begin A
New Work/Mission

Many pastors would like to start a new work or adopt a struggling church, but don't know how. As an addendum to Chapter 7, "Make A Great Commotion About The Great Commission," here are a few practical steps on how to accomplish them both.

1. Locate an area in need of a church: in a new and growing suburb, an ethnic neighborhood, or inner-city area that has been neglected.

2. Find a suitable place to meet for Bible study and worship: in a store-front building, a home, a mobile chapel, a vacated church, your own church, or new mission building.

3. Engage leadership to visit, teach, preach in the new mission, i.e., a young minister, retired pastor, lay-leader, or bi-vocational pastor.

4. Provide the necessary funds for rent, mortgage payments, utilities, literature, supplies, salaries, insurance and retirement.

5. Then go for it! Our church began as a mission in a new suburb in 1955, and one of the reasons it has thrived is that it was born well. New churches, like newborn children, need a strong start.

Adopt a Church

Many growing and/or ethnic neighborhoods need new churches,

while struggling churches in changing neighborhoods need strengthening.

Here's how.

1. When you meet with the pastor or deacons of a struggling church, or through your associational director of missions, make them aware that you would like to adopt the church in need. Normally, there will be no interest unless the situation is desperate.

2.   Should the church wish to be adopted, meet with the congregation to clearly outline the conditions of adoption. These are the conditions I outlined for our four adopted churches at Green Acres:

a.   Church management would be handed over to a joint committee consisting of two members of the mission and three members of the adopting church.   Failing congregations have problems with leadership.   Sometimes, its leaders are old, other times, leadership lacks vision or are too negative.

Committee leadership frees the church and new pastor from the old power structure and provides new, progressive attitudes necessary for the reclamation and growth of the church.

b.   The property is deeded to the adopting church. Because the adopting church is providing a new pastor, paying his moving expenses, renovating the property, and placing workers in the church, the adopting church needs full control.   This way, a congregation can't change its mind and revert to independent status.

c.   The mission retains its mission status until Sunday school attendance consistently reaches 200. This is an arbitrary number, but a proven one.

The goal for an adopted congregation is to regain independence and to become self-supporting again—when it's ready. If churches break adoption ties too soon, they often revert to old ways quickly.

d.   Members of the mission become members of the adopting church with all rights and privileges, including access to youth and family centers, participation in all sports and church activities, etc.

e.   Mission churches need fresh leadership: teachers, musicians, choir members, etc. Members of the adopting congregation can infuse new life into a mission church by serving as leaders in these areas; many will stay.

f. Those who begin attending the mission give their tithe to the mission; this gives immediate, increased financial strength to the mission church.

g. A staff member, usually the Minister of Special Ministries, preaches at the church for six to nine months. This helps the mission church clearly identify with the adopting church, provides adequate time for an attitude change before a new minister takes over, and saves the expense of a pastor's salary during the early recuperative period.

h. Repair and shape-up the facility and add a new sign. This impression of newness helps when newspaper advertising is initiated.

i. When a new pastor is chosen, the adopting church determines the candidates, the congregation gives the approvals. The new pastor becomes part of the adopting church staff under their supervision. This way, the new pastor has help establishing priorities for his ministry: visitation expectations, preaching responsibilities, a minimum of administrative duties, planning a calendar, setting growth goals, living within a budget. The pastor is also accountable to the adopting church for the overall work and progress of the mission church.

The adopting church helps its mission church and new pastor by providing: support, fellowship and encouragement through the entire staff; a wealth of resources relative to music, Sunday school, buildings, maintenance, finances, office equipment; all financial transactions.

Appendix II

Evangelistic Churches Care For Their Staff

Woodrow Wilson's father, a Presbyterian minister, was driving his buggy one day, pulled by a beautiful, sleek mare. A deacon saw him and asked, "Why is it, Brother Wilson, that your mare looks so fine and you look so poorly?"

"That's easy," the Reverend Wilson said, "I care for the mare, and you care for me."

Concerning pastor selection, someone once remarked: "When a church seeks a pastor, they look for a man with the strength of an eagle, the grace of a swan, the gentleness of a dove, the friendliness of a sparrow, and the night hours of an owl. And, when they find that bird, they expect him to live on the food of a canary."

Things have improved in recent years, but historically, churches have been notorious for paying low salaries and awarding small benefits to their pastors and staffs. However, that is not the way of great evangelistic churches, for great churches realize that no organization rises above their leadership. So they love, respect, and fairly compensate their staffs.

That's part of what makes these churches great. Moreover, great evangelistic churches build their ministry around the Bible, and the Scriptures state that churches have a spiritual duty to care for the financial needs of their leaders. Speaking of the church's duty to its pastor, the apostle Paul said, "Let the elders [those appointed to take spiritual charge of churches] that rule well be counted worthy of double honour [honorarium/pay], especially they who labour in the word and doctrine" (1 Timothy 5:17).

Paul makes it clear that those who preach and teach, those who work to edify and build the church by preaching the truth to its people, and those who educate the young and new converts in the Christian way, must be adequately paid. Paul reinforces this principle by quoting both the Old Testament and the words of Jesus: "For the scripture saith, 'Thou shalt not muzzle the ox that treadeth out the corn'" and "The laborer is worthy of his reward" (1 Timothy 5:18). Paul, of course, recalls Deuteronomy (25:4) and Luke (10:7) in his epistle to Timothy and, another time, echoes the same sentiments to the Corinthians (1 Corinthians 9:4-14).

In an earlier passage in the letter to Timothy, Paul talks generally about care and provision: "But if any provide not for his own, and specially for those of his own house, he hath denied the faith, and is worse than an infidel" (1 Timothy 5:8). The bottom line is, the needs of those who toil should be recognized and their labors rewarded, i.e., the minister and his staff.

Here, the Greek word translated provide means to plan ahead for a future event, to give forethought to, to look beyond today.

Clearly, we have a spiritual duty to provide for the material and financial needs of our families. But, how can a pastor do this if his church does not provide adequately for him? To provide for those under them is both a church and an individual responsibility. What, then, should a church do to fulfill its spiritual obligation? How can we do, in a practical way, what the scriptures say to do?

An Extra Benefit/Adequate Annuity

First of all, I would suggest that a church strive to match ten percent of its pastor's salary as an added benefit and place it in the Church Annuity Plan. This helps to prepare a minister for old age, so that he may conduct his ministerial duties without concern for his material needs.

A Personal Responsibility

A minister should strive to add five percent to his plan. With a total of 15 percent set aside, the amount available at retirement would be adequate, if started early enough.

Cooperative Agreement

If the church will enter into a cooperative agreement with the state convention, up to an additional $35.00 per month may be provided for the minister. Half this amount—or $17.50—provides for survivor benefits of up to $67,000 term life insurance and as much as $300 per month disability insurance. The remaining $17.50 is applied to the minister's personal retirement income account.

Term Life Insurance

To protect itself, the church should also provide adequate term life insurance for its ministers and staff. The cost is low and the protection

Health Insurance

Every person needs adequate health coverage in the face of rapidly escalating medical costs.

Notes

Preface
> *Reader's Digest*, "Personal Glimpses," May, 1987, p. 70.

Chapter 5
> Schuller, Robert H., *Self Esteem, The New Reformation*, Word Books, 1982, p. 103. Only a portion of the poem is included in Schuller's book; it is undocumented.

Chapter 6
> *The Criswell Study Bible*, Thomas Nelson Publishers, 1979. Footnote on Hebrews 3:7.
> Hobbs, Herschel, "Baptist Beliefs," *Baptist Standard*, July 27, 1988, p. 7.

Chapter 9
> Dukahonchenka, Jacob, *The Commission*, August, 1984: Irwin, James B. *More Than Earthlings*, Broadman Press, 1983, p. 21.
> Manchester, William, *The Lost Lion,* Winston Spencer Churchill, *Alone 1932-1940*. Little, Brown, 1988.

Chapter 10
> Baxter, Richard, "Frail, but Effective," Warren W. Wiersbe, Moody Monthly, January 1976.
> Chadwick, Samuel, *Salvation*, Lewis Sperry Chafer, Moody Press, 1944.
> Graham, Billy, "Foolishness of Preaching," Moody Monthly.
> Pollard, Frank, *After You've Said I'm Sorry*, Broadman Press, 1982.